The In(ter)vention of the Hay(na)ku

Selected Tercets 1996-2019

BY EILEEN R. TABIOS

POETRY

After The Egyptians Determined The Shape of the World Is A Circle, 1996
Beyond Life Sentences, 1998
The Empty Flagpole (CD with guest artist Mei-mei Berssenbrugge), 2000
Ecstatic Mutations (with short stories and essays), 2001
Reproductions of The Empty Flagpole, 2002
Enheduanna in the 21st Century, 2002
There, Where the Pages Would End, 2003
Menage a Trois With the 21st Century, 2004
Crucial Bliss Epilogues, 2004
The Estrus Gaze(s), 2005
Songs of the Colon, 2005
Post Bling Bling, 2005
I Take Thee, English, For My Beloved, 2005
The Secret Lives of Punctuations, Vol. I, 2006
Dredging for Atlantis, 2006
It's Curtains, 2006
SILENCES: The Autobiography of Loss, 2007
The Singer and Others: Flamenco Hay(na)ku, 2007
The Light Sang As It Left Your Eyes: Our Autobiography, 2007
Nota Bene Eiswein, 2009
Footnotes to Algebra: Uncollected Poems 1995-2009, 2009
On A Pyre: An Ars Poetica, 2010
Roman Holiday, 2010
Hay(na)ku for Haiti, 2010
THE THORN ROSARY: Selected Prose Poems and New 1998-2010, 2010
the relational elations   of ORPHANED ALGEBRA (with j/j hastain), 2012
5 Shades of Gray, 2012
THE AWAKENING: A Long Poem Triptych & A Poetics Fragment, 2013
147 Million Orphans (MMXI-MML), 2014
44 RESURRECTIONS, 2014
SUN STIGMATA (Sculpture Poems), 2014
I Forgot Light Burns, 2015
Duende in the Alleys, 2015
INVENT(ST)ORY: Selected Catalog Poems & New (1996-2015), 2015
The Connoisseur of Alleys, 2016
The Gilded Age of Kickstarters, 2016
Excavating the Filipino in Me, 2016
I Forgot Ars Poetica, 2016
AMNESIA: Somebody's Memoir, 2016

THE OPPOSITE OF CLAUSTROPHOBIA: Prime's Anti-Autobiography, 2017
Post-Ecstasy Mutations, 2017
On Green Lawn, The Scent of White, 2017
To Be An Empire Is To Burn, 2017
If They Hadn't Worn White Hoods ... (with John Bloomberg-Rissman), 2017
What Shivering Monks Comprehend, 2017
YOUR FATHER IS BALD: Selected Hay(na)ku Poems, 2017
IMMIGRANT: Hay(na)ku & Other Poems In A New Land, 2017
Comprehending Mortality (with John Bloomberg-Rissman), 2017
Big City Cante Intermedio, 2017
WINTER ON WALL STREET: A Novella-in-Verse, 2017
Making National Poetry Month Great Again, 2017
MANHATTAN: An Archaeology, 2017
Love In A Time of Belligerence, 2017
MURDER DEATH RESURRECTION: A Poetry Generator, 2018
TANKA, Vol. I, 2018
HIRAETH: Tercets From The Last Archipelago, 2018
One, Two, Three: Selected Hay(na)ku Poems (Trans. Rebeka Lembo), 2018
THE GREAT AMERICAN NOVEL: Selected Visual Poetry 2001-2019, 2019
The In(ter)vention of the Hay(na)ku: Selected Tercets 1996-2019, 2019
Witness in the Convex Mirror, 2019
EVOCARE: Collected Tanka (with Ayo Gutierrez and Brian Cain Aene), 2019
WE ARE IT, 2019
Drawings Form/From the Six Directions, 2019

FICTION

Behind The Blue Canvas, 2004
Novel Chatelaine, 2009
SILK EGG: Collected Novels 2009-2009, 2011

PROSE COLLECTIONS

Black Lightning: Poetry-In-Progress (poetry essays/interviews), 1998
My Romance (art essays with poems), 2002
The Blind Chatelaine's Keys (biography with haybun), 2008
AGAINST MISANTHROPY: A Life in Poetry (2015-1995), 2015
#EileenWritesNovel, 2017

The In(ter)vention of the Hay(na)ku

Selected Tercets 1996-2019

Eileen R. Tabios

Marsh Hawk Press, 2019

ISBN: 978-0-9969911-6-2

First edition 10 9 8 7 5 6 5 4 3 2

Marsh Hawk Press books are published by Marsh Hawk Press, Inc., a not-for-
profit corporation under section 501©3 United States Internal Revenue
Code.

Book design by Michelle M. Bautista

Cover art: Treva Tabios, "Drowning" (2018), 24" x 36". Acrylic on canvas. The
painting is from her "Haiku to Canvas" series. "Drowning" also enabled her
to write her own tercet, the following haiku:

"Drowning"

The air is humid
A churning in the stomach
Memories fade black

Names: Tabios, Eileen, author.
Title: The in(ter)vention of the hay(na)ku : selected tercets, 1996-2019 /
  Eileen R. Tabios.
Description: First edition. | East Rockaway : Marsh Hawk Press, 2019.
Identifiers: LCCN 2019008869 | ISBN 9780996991162 (pbk.)
Classification: LCC PS3570.A234 A6 2019 | DDC 811/.54--dc23 LC record
available at https://lccn.loc.gov/2019008869

Marsh Hawk Press
P.O. Box 206, East Rockaway, NY 11518-0206
www.marshhawkpress.org

ACKNOWLEDGMENTS

Deep gratitude as ever to Marsh Hawk Press, especially to Thomas Fink, Sandy McIntosh, and Burt Kimmelman. As well, thanks to Michelle Bautista for book design and Treva Tabios for cover art work.

Individual works in this collection were previously published in the following books and chapbooks, as well as anthologies, journals, and online spaces—thank you to their editors/curators and publishers:

POEMS
Books & Chapbooks:
[The Table of Contents features which poems are published in which books.]

After the Egyptians Determined The Shape of the World is a Circle (Pometaphysics Publishing, Lutherville, MD, 1996)

Beyond Life Sentences (Anvil Publishing, Philippines, 1998)

Dredging for Atlantis (Otoliths, Australia, 2006)

Footnotes to Algebra: Uncollected Poems 1995-2009 (BlazeVOX Books, New York, 2009)

Hay(na)ku for Haiti (Meritage Press, San Francisco, 2010)

I Take Thee, English, For My Beloved (Marsh Hawk Press, New York, 2005)

Menage A Trois With the 21st Century (xPress(ed), Finland, 2004)

Nota Bene Eiswein (ahadada books, Tokyo & Toronto, 2009)

On Green Lawn, The Scent of White (Poems-For-All, San Diego, 2017)

The Light Sang As It Left Your Eyes: Our Autobiography (Marsh Hawk Press, New York, 2007)

The Singer and Others: Flamenco Hay(na)ku (Dusie, Switzerland, 2007)

Your Father Is Bald: Selected Hay(na)ku Poems (Trilingual, Limited Edition in English, Romanian and Spanish. Pim Publishing House's "Bibliotheca Universalis" Collection, Romania, 2017)

One, Two, Three: Selected Hay(na)ku Poems / Uno, dos, tres: Selección de Hay(na)kus (Bilingual edition with Spanish Translator Rebeka Lembo. Paloma Press, San Mateo, 2018)

Journals & Online Spaces:
ANO BA ZINE; ars poetica; Big City Lit; The Brooklyn Rail; CRITIPHORIA; Dragonfire; First Annual Festival of Women's Poetry/Wompherence; Inertia Magazine; The Journal of Commonwealth & Postcolonial Studies; Litter Magazine (Leafe Press); THE MARGINS (Asian American Writers Workshop)*; Marsh Hawk Review; Muddy River Poetry Review; Otoliths: A Magazine of Many E-Things; Our Own Voice; PEEP/SHOW: A Taxonomic Exercise in Textual and Visual Seriality; Watermelon Isotope; What Rough Beast (Indolent Books);* and *WordWrights*

Anthologies:
"Athena," "The Bread of Florence," and "The Hay(na)ku of Numbers"—*THE HAY(NA)KU ANTHOLOGY, VOL. II*, Editors Jean Vengua and Mark Young (Meritage Press / xPress(ed), San Francisco & Saint Helena / Finland, 2008)

"Die We Do"—*FIELD OF MIRRORS: An Anthology of Philippine American Writers*, Editor Edwin Lozada (Philippine American Writers & Artists, Inc., San Francisco, 2008)

"Ferdinand Edralin Marcos (Rippled Mirror Hay(na)ku #1)"—*Resist Much / Obey Little*, Editors Michael Boughn, John Bradley, Brenda Cardenas, Ching-In Chen, Lynne DeSilva-Johnson, Kass Fleisher, Roberto Harrison, Kent Johnson, Andrew Levy, Nathaniel Mackey, Ruben Medina, Philip Metres, Nita Noveno, Julie Patton, Margaret Randall, Michael Rothenberg, Anne Waldman and Tyrone Williams (Spuyten Duyvil Press and Dispatches Editions, New York, 2017)

"Four Skin Confessions"—*The Chained Hay(na)ku Project*, Editors Ivy Alvarez, John Bloomberg-Rissman, Ernesto Priego and Eileen R. Tabios (Meritage Press / xPress(ed), San Francisco & St. Helena / Finland, 2012)

"Hay Naku! That Menopause!"—*Menopausal Hay(na)ku for P-Grubbers*, Editor Eileen R. Tabios (Locofo Chaps/Moria Books, Chicago, 2017)

"Ifugao Red"—*Saints of Hysteria: A Half Century of Collaborative Poetry*, Editors Denise Duhamel, Maureen Seaton and David Trinidad (Soft Skull Press, Brooklyn, 2007)

"Ifugao Red"—*E-X-C-H-A-N-G-E-V-A-L-U-E-S: the first XI interviews*, Editor Tom Beckett (Otoliths, Australia, 2007)

"Maganda Begins"—*Kuwento: Lost Things*, Editors Rachelle Cruz & Melissa Sipin (Carayan Press, San Francisco, 2014)

"Tercets From the Book of Revelations"—*LANGUAGE FOR A NEW CENTURY:*

Contemporary Poetry From The Middle East, Asia and Beyond, Editors Tina Chang, Nathalie Handal and Ravi Shankar (W.W. Norton & Company, New York et al, 2008)

"Girl Singing: The Secret Life of an Angel" was featured in *1,000 More Views of 'Girl Singing'* (Leafe Press, U.K., 2009), an anthology edited by John Bloomberg-Rissman which features nearly 40 poets and visual artists creating new work in response to the poem. The anthology itself has been used several times as a writing prompt for students of Rupert Loydell at Falmouth University

"Maganda Begins"—*The World I Leave You: Asian American Poets on Faith and Spirit*, Editors Leah Silvieus and Lee Herrick (Orison Books, Asheville, 2020)

"Venus Rising For The First Time in the 21st Century"—*Times New Roman: Poets Oppose 21st Century Empire*, ed. Todd Swift (Nthposition.com, 2003)

"Weather Du Jour," "Die We Do," "The Hay(na)ku of Numbers," and excerpts from "The Ineffability of Mushrooms"—*BARDS OF THE FAR EAST: Anthology of Haiku and Kindred Verses*, Editor-Authors Carolyn Gutierrez-Abanggan, Ligaw Makata, Jose Rizal Reyes, Felix Fojas and Danny Gallardo (Philippines, 2017)

ESSAY

"The History of the Hay(na)ku" (in varying versions) was previously published in the following anthologies:

HAY(NA)KU 15, Editor Eileen R. Tabios (Meritage Press / Paloma Press / xPress(ed), San Francisco & St. Helena / San Mateo / Finland and with sponsors San Francisco Public Library's Filipino American Center and Philippine American Writers & Artists, 2018)

A TRANSPACIFIC POETICS, Editors Lisa Samuels and Sawako Nakayasu (Litmus Press, Brooklyn, 2017)

THE HAY(NA)KU ANTHOLOGY, VOL. II, Editors Jean Vengua and Mark Young (Meritage Press / xPress(ed), San Francisco & St Helena / Finland, 2008)

THE FIRST HAY(NA)KU ANTHOLOGY, Editors Jean Vengua and Mark Young (Meritage Press / xPress(ed), San Francisco & St Helena / Finland, 2005)

OTHER

"Mudra" was written for "Clit Chat," a Bastos, Inc. Production presented at Bindlestiff Studios, San Francisco, February 14-16, 2002. "Mudra" was also part of a "Poetry Mobile Project" curated by *Our Own Voice* for exhibit at a George Washington University (GWU) Book Fair. The GWU Fair was part of the "October Heritage Series 2004 Salute to Filipino Authors" sponsored by the Cultural Affairs Division of the Philippine Embassy held October 15-17, 2004 in Washington D.C.

Part 4 of "The Ineffability of Mushrooms" was featured—under the title "Truffle Hounds"—as a poetry broadside for a "Paw-etry Reading & Reception" at Half Moon Bay Library (California); the April 14, 2019 event was a fundraiser for the Peninsula Humane Society & SPCA. The poem was selected by San Mateo Poet Laureate Aileen Cassinetto.

Thomas Fink's introductory essay was first published in *Otoliths*.

CONTENTS

II. HAY(NA)KU

II. MURDER DEATH RESURRECTION (MDR), 2014-2018

IV. DEATH POEMS, 2018-2019

Author's Note

I create "Selected Poems" based on poetic form as it allows me—and readers—to see if I contribute to expanding the form's possibilities. In the case of the tercet, my contribution is the "hay(na)ku."

I also present my poems in the chronological order of when they were written and published. I do so because Poetry is also a process, and the chronological presentation of the work can reveal something about the poet's interests or inclinations that eventually led to an invention of the hay(na)ku.

I have grouped the poems in four sections. The first section presents tercets before I invented the hay(na)ku. The second section presents hay(na)ku in its varied forms. The third section presents hay(na)ku which emanated from another project, "Murder, Death and Resurrection" (MDR). An essay explaining MDR is also included, and the reader may notice how MDR is dependent on reader engagement to write—not interpret, but to write— the poem. Such space for the reader has always been part of the hay(na)ku, which has led other poets and artists around the world to create numerous variations of the hay(na)ku's basic tercet form.

In the fourth section, I include two poetic approaches for contrast. The first poem, "Dear A, This Poem Is Not For You," presents tercets where each line is a complete sentence. This sentence-based poem is more maximalist than the typical hay(na)ku that contains mostly short lines. The second element is a hay(na)ku series inspired by the death poem genre developed in East Asian cultures, "Hay(na)ku Death Poems."

I hope the reader finds something illuminating if not enjoyable about the tercet form in my practice.

Eileen R. Tabios
April 14, 2019
Saint Helena

INTRODUCTION

By Thomas Fink

Evidently, Dante invented *terza rima* to write *The Divine Comedy*. It may be the first example in the West of a poetic form based on tercets, whereas the haiku appeared slightly earlier—in thirteenth century Japan, though it was popularized by Basho much later. The title, *The In(ter)vention of the Hay(na)ku: Selected Tercets 1996-2019,* informs us that Eileen Tabios' method of assembling a collection is to foreground both her invention of the form, which has intervened in contemporary poetic practice for the last sixteen years by providing a new formal alternative (a tercet with one word in the first line, two in the second, three in the third), and her non-hay(na)ku poems that utilize tercets without counting words or scramble the order of the hay(na)ku count.

One of Tabios' previous Selected volumes used prose-poetry as the framing device, and many readers first encountered her prose-poetry—for example, in *Reproductions of the Empty Flagpole* (Marsh Hawk Press, 2002)—before they read much or any of her work in verse. And she has written a great deal of prose-poetry throughout her career. This point deserves attention because the tercet is shaped so differently than the paragraph, and so we can expect some aesthetic effects to differ markedly.

The rationale for a large collection of tercets makes sense in a way that one of quatrains or couplets would not, because Tabios *did* dream up the hay(na)ku. But a poet who makes this decision runs the risk of formal monotony. Here, Tabios overcomes this risk by demonstrating several variations within the use of the tercet. This happens right away. The first poem in *The In(ter)vention*, "listening to what woke me," initially published in her debut volume in 1996, has long, punctuationless lines, one dependent or independent clause to a line, and in the middle, a tercet that behaves like William Carlos Williams' triadic/stepped lines, a late career innovation, and finally, a monostich. The third poem, "Mortality," returns to the long lines of "listening to what woke me," but has a great deal of punctuation. The second poem, "Anticipating Siberia" features medium-sized lines with punctuation; like "Mortality," many of these lines have a strong pause, while a few are enjambed. And then we come to "Venus Rising for the First Time in the 21st Century," where an anticipatory glimpse of the hay(na) ku's spare quality becomes discernible:

You want to see
her seeing
herself. You want

her seeing
her wanting
you behind the wave

foaming
when you become
the sea seeing

her eyes form
(above a body you
dreamt into salt water)

to see you
through strands
of dark seaweed.

In short-lined tercets like these, which only occasionally "balloon" to five
words in a line, the play of enjambment and caesura often becomes a
central component in the poem's temporal unfolding, and it is not only
enjambment within a tercet but between them. Poetic thought/perception
proceeds sinuously, sometimes hesitantly, without rushing. (And when these
elements are less dominant in a tercet-poem or hay(na)ku-based text, as
in parts of "Enheduanna #20," which I will discuss shortly, it creates a
sharper, *less* consistently exploratory effect and more of a succession of
bursts.)

Apart from the formal effects I have just addressed, a new collection of
Tabios' work from the beginning of her writing life to the present should
yield a solid sense of the problematics and topoi that she has consistently
tackled. The lines above from "Venus Rising for the First Time in the
21st Century" provide a fine example of what Joi Barrios, placing Tabios'
work in relation to feminist Filipina bardic precursors, identifies as a major
thematic dimension: "Tabios' poems seemingly speak of love and desire,
and yet are powerful statements that participate in discourses on gender,
class, and power" (318). As it interacts playfully with the trope of "sea"
that points to the mythological context of Venus' birth, the repetition of
"see," as well as "want," involving a "you" (male gazer) and "her" (the 21st

century Venus) can be said to interrogate the power of the male onlooker to establish contexts of perception. According to this interpretation, the "you" seems to want Venus to experience a kind of "double consciousness" (W.E.B. DuBois' term applied to African-Americans early in the twentieth century) so that she can participate in and accept her own objectification rather than experience her (new) life in an unmediated way, and he wishes to *witness* it—as reassurance that it is happening. Yet the second sentence, beginning at the end of the first tercet with the same words that started off the poem, indicate the male's desire for her to be conscious of her desire for him. Interestingly, though, the man figures himself not as traditional masculine solidity but as a "body" of water, a "form" of "foam," and this troping suggests the tenuousness of the male's desire, the fragility that threatens his social power. Tabios' speaker declares that the male addressee aims

to commence
a vision you
have shared with her

in her (lurking unknowingly)
through her
seeing you....

Prepositions merit attention here: while "with" implies mutuality of desire called up by the verb "have shared," as well as acknowledgment of Venus' agency, "in" can mean the man's aggressive invasion, and "through" can suggest her seeing as something utilized for his own self-regard. A few lines later, there is more wordplay with "see": see(d)ing you/ sea-ing her/ seeing you." "See(d)ing" is a loaded signifier, because, although it is generally associated (literally) with patriarchal power, the power of insemination, the action of her seeing is engendering his vision, perhaps suggesting that she does possess agency, the power of subjectivity, and is not merely an "object" evincing beauty.

Barrios articulates the feminist disclosure of female power in "the Enheduanna poems of *Menage a Trois with the 21st Century*" (2004), in which "Tabios privileges the woman's voice and even when she speaks of the man longed for—'you'—it is from the woman's imagined perspective.... What really matters is the woman imagining 'you'" (320) and not the actual "you," whatever or whoever that is. In "Enheduanna #20," the sole poem selected for *The In(ter)vention of the Hay(na)ku: Selected Tercets*, and another tercet-poem with relatively short lines, two opening questions compel a recognition of the speaker's influence over the man as she seeks to fathom his prediction about specifics of his future subjectivity: "As you fall asleep/ in my skin/ will you dream?// Will you want/ you or want/ to change?" Then again, Barrios might be right that this "is from the woman's imagined perspective," since the speaker's apostrophic questions cannot be answered by a "you" who exists, if he exists, outside the poem. After some questioning of herself, she returns to questioning him:

Will you bring the scent
of red roses
I left behind

in New York City alleyways
(or has that season yet to pass)?
In my eyes

will you see
Baudelaire's infinity
he defined as the "sky"

you witness repeatedly
on and in any painting
marked by blue sapphire, lapis

lazuli, indigo, turquoise...sky...?

Far from acquiescence to male social power, this questioning, whether rhetorical or actual, uses the tropes of courtship and seduction—not to valorize them, but to explore the psychology of desire and power relations in ways that do not assume the eventual dominance of either party. And sometimes, when the poet casts aside these tropes, we encounter an urgent directness made all the more urgent and direct by the hay(na)ku's formal simplicity and compactness:

My love. If
words can
reach

whatever world you
suffer in—
Listen:

I have things
to tell
you.

The speaker at year's end seems at first to speak of physical contact, this turns out to be her imagination, which she labels "violent": "I prowl/ somber streets/ holding// you—in my/ head, this/ violence!—//a violent gaze./ You." The headnote of this 2007 poem "Maganda Begins" serves as a salient social frame: "'Maganda' is not just a Tagalog word that means 'beautiful.' 'Maganda' is also the name of the first woman in a Filipino creation myth."

As Tabios has herself in explanatory pieces and in titling a large brick of a book, *I Take Thee, English, for My Beloved* (2005), Joi Barrios, Leny Mendoza Strobel, and other feminist Filipina critics have underlined the relationship in her poetry between the representation of erotic interchange and the power dynamics of colonial and postcolonial subjects and those entities who have imposed not only "a violent gaze" but violent constraints on their political, economic, and cultural agency. One might hypothesize that Maganda is not addressing her "love" in the "present" of creation but a distant future, our present. From this perspective, "I have things/ to tell" not only a "you" who has "suffered" in the "world" of the twenty-first century Philippines and the Filipino/a diaspora, whether male, female, or gender-neutral, but a (post)colonial figure who has gained the speaker's erotic attention. English itself is "spoken" in the poem by Maganda, and the language might also be considered a possible addressee, as I find Anny Ballardini accurate in referring to "Tabios' "passionate 'love-hate' bondage with the English language" developing "in nuances that reach both extremes: passionate eroticism and annihilation by alternating supplications and requests... (19).

In the Enheduanna poems, Ric Carfagna finds the speakers in Tabios' poems "at times to be entranced, totally absorbed in 'otherness'" (35), and it is important to reiterate that this is not capitulation to the dominance of an other, but an interrogation of possibilities of intersubjectivity, as in the opening lines of the 2006 "Burning Pulpit," a poem that conflates erotic and religious intensity: *Could/ our two miseries/ copulate into one opulent being?*" This powerful question is followed by a snappy critique of a typical patriarchal strategy that would stand in the way of "opulent being": "Men simplify/ then slink back/ to antediluvian burrows."

Another gender-themed tercet poem "Hay Naku! That Menopause!" (2017) wittily and fiercely tackles a subject that many men might choose to minimize:

Men—
O pause:
Reconsider, then begin....

Men—
O pause:
On the other

hand
I feel
quite proud of

my
hot flashes.

And why is menopause a source of pride? "*I feel amazed/ over/ generating so/ much heat,*" as though she could// *absolutely/ warm up/ an entire city!*" The enjambments foreground both words conveying energy and small directional words that convey conduits for the movement of that energy. A later section of the poem offers a less jocular recontextualization of a negative to a positive: Tabios insists that "men" "pause" in their "concern" for Angelina Jolie that, in removing her "ovaries and// breasts," "she// might enter menopause/ early," while the actress pushes "back/ against the narrative" of "menopause" as "unwelcome" and "aging" as "bad."

Another prominent thematic terrain in *The In(ter)vention of the Hay(na)ku: Selected Tercets* involves theorizing about poetry *within* the poems. While this could prove a dull, mechanical exercise, Tabios does not so much philosophize abstractly as underscore a sense of necessity, as in "Poetics (#1):

What we wanted
to do
to be

was what we were *helpless*
against doing
against being

The parallel structure in the last two (two-word) lines of each tercet not only animates the sense of "helplessness" but also points to the notion that "to do" is preferable to being "against doing," and "to be" authentically contrasts mightily with being "against being." (It is a tough position, after all, to be "against being.")

"As If" captures Tabios making fun of the hubris she has exhibited in believing her own prior dictum, "'If a poem/ is so/ powerful// it will return....'" She tells of a situation where she received linguistic inspiration and did not choose to write down the lines, and "it feels like/ years and/ yet// that poem has/ not yet/ returned." This little narrative placed in a reverse hay(na)ku format playfully echoes Socrates' distaste for the new technology of writing as a threat to the cultivation of memory and to the full power of primordial speech.

In "Athena" Tabios ponders the complexities of poetic revision:

What's deemed necessary
changes. Hear
me

listening in another
decade, editing
last

and first lines.
A different
Singer

croons from behind
an impassive
speaker.

Tabios can speak of "a different/ Singer," despite the fact that the same poet is reviewing the poem "in another/ decade," evidently because she believes that new preoccupations have transformed her. She finds a different sense of necessity in her lines—probably an unanticipated context—as she renews the editing process. "The poem cannot/ be pure" for various reasons, but here, it signifies that the poem cannot be "purely" fixed in the mind of its writer and first reader because later experiences and insights coloring subsequent readings will change its meanings and impact for her: "Sound// never travels unimpeded/ by anonymous/ butterflies." And of course, "butterflies" do not stick around long in one's visual field. Indeed, "writing it down/ merely freezes/ flight" temporarily because further reader-response, which the poet calls "translation," will reactivate the motion of a fresh encounter with the text. Even a seemingly stable vision is subject to sharp displacement: "The sky/ ruptured/ suddenly—" In this spirit, Ballardini praises "Tabios' words and continuous twists" for catching "the reader with their luring beauty to flee as soon as they have reached him" (18).

Tabios' "Death Poems" tend to use small words with maximum acuity: "Die We Do" packs a great deal into three hay(na)kus:

Die
we do
as much as

we
live. Then
we write: right

what
we lived
when we write.

The first sentence cannot be about temporal quantity, since, if no other incarnations are factored in, the amount of time being dead is not equal to the amount being alive. Therefore, perhaps the first sentence is an assessment of equality of significance between the two elements in the opposition. Another possibility is to link the verb "die" to the life-long process of moving toward death. However, the last five lines might tilt the poem in a different direction: in writing, re-presenting "life," "we" writers "kill" "what we lived"; to "right" it as we see fit may be to "wrong" what happened in the execution of a set of intentions designed to validate the self to others and itself.

The numbered "Hay(na)ku Death Poems, all of which are "written in the 'reverse'… form to visually manifest disappearance," manifest divergent perspectives on death. #2 rejoices in Proustian memory-triggers: "Familiar, joyous barking—/ we'll meet/ again," and #14 subtly suggests the redemptive power of poetry, including brief poems: "Against silence, even/ haiku are/ maximalists." On the other hand, #4 through #6 lament the appearance of veins as harbingers of demise: "Veins rippling protests—/ rivers into/ Hades" (#4). Speaking of the death of a bird against a windexed-windowpane, #15 ends with a jab against "cruel// hypocrisy in creating/

this bloody/ Anthropocene." The equally thorough bleakness of #7 is perhaps balanced by the indeterminacy of whether "Grief overcomes/ joy" for the dying or living onlookers, and the next deathbed poem (#8) seems a rebuke to Catholics who believe that last rites confer absolution:

To be human
is to
sin.

But knowledge is
no palliative
upon

reaching one's deathbed

For Eileen Tabios, "to be human/ is to" write and read variously, among other things. An assessment of the scope of Tabios' poetic accomplishment would require a comparative perusal of this Selected Tercets, her Selected Prose Poems, her Selected Catalog Poems, her Selected Visual Poetry, texts in other verse-forms, and her forays into computer-inspired poetry, some of which appear herein, as well as other aspects of what has been called "Conceptual Poetry." That being said, it is evident that ample multeity exists within the boundaries of this In(ter)vention.

WORKS CITED

Ballardini, Anny. "Eileen Tabios and the Upturning of Codified Needs." The Blind Chatelaine's Keys: Her Autobiography through Your Poetics. Blazevox, 2008, pp. 18-24.

Barrios, Joi. "Afterword: Fearless Peerless Kasu-Kasuan Poetry." Tabios. The Thorn Rosary: Selected Prose Poems and New (1998-2010). Marsh Hawk Press, 2010, pp. 313-322.

Carafagna, Ric. "Let Us Now Praise Famous Women…." The Blind Chatelaine's Keys: Her Autobiography through Your Poetics. Blazevox, 2008, pp. 32-39.

Thomas Fink is the author of *A Different Sense of Power: Problems of Community in Late Twentieth Century U.S. Poetry* (2001) and co-editor of two collections of essays, including *Reading the Difficulties: Dialogues with Innovative American Poetry* (2014). His criticism has been published in Contemporary Literature, American Poetry Review, Jacket 2, Verse, and numerous other publications. He has published nine books of poetry, most recently *Selected Poems & Poetic Series* (2016).

I. SELECTED TERCETS

to bring
a poem
into the world

is to bring
the world
into a poem

        —Eileen R. Tabios

.

From *After the Egyptians Determined The Shape of the World is a Circle*, 1996

listening to what woke me

in the city, as summer evaporates off the streets
the stilled, sharp blades of a three-pronged fan
behind the curve of its grated metal mask

the fragments of dust wakened
by the sole of a gavel
slamming as the judge stands

the pale-pink cotton fluttering
from a baby's tiny snore
no nightmares cracking the eggshell of her brow

a memory of Black Mesa (New Mexico), an infinite sapphire
past the horizon as we drive by in a red car, windows open
drifting with the smoke in Anita's song

your finger
        trailing the ragged seam
                        of my belly's stretchmark

the last puddle of spicy, flour-thickened gravy
as a crumbling piece of warm cornbread
hovers, the butter dripping

you cannot translate the scattered remnants of a circle
covering the box from Chinatown in the hands of a wrinkled uncle
and I think of moths as the sun disappears

—the flutter of wings as they tease a dim porch light

From Beyond Life Sentences, 1998

Anticipating Siberia

I hear the birth of rain, see
a tree bow from its burden:
clouds weeping on stolid leaves.

Lake Baikal freezes when winter
capes Siberia. But the buried fishes,
I am convinced, do not shiver.

A Bowery drunk smashes an empty bottle,
gasps, "Come on, come on!"
to the serial killer sloppy that night.

Men leave. Women leave.
Men die. Women die. A door opens.
Sometimes, an end is still the best conclusion.

Amsterdam or London—the layover
will not matter when I arrive
in St. Petersburg to depart on a train

whose conductors yell to milling crowds:
"Irkuts!" I can smell the mint of the tea
steaming from porcelain between my hands.

Mortality

Your father irritates me—he walks like an old man,
she says, though my father exists in the same room.
Then my mother waits expectantly for my response.

I refuse to rise to the bait, stare at my wedding photo
on top of the piano whose keys have settled into a graveyard:
I marvel I once was a girl with plump lips and cheekbones.

She won't let go: *All he does is eat and sleep, sleep and eat—*
like he's become a new-born. I'm not his mother!
She adds though he stares, unblinking, at her.

Dad, would you like something to drink?
I ask as I stand to deflect my mother by pretending
I am thirsty, though I know there is nothing in their house

to fulfill me. My mother frowns, then sniffs, as I refuse
to address her concerns. I avoid looking into her eyes
where I know tears are ready to spring.

My father blinks before uttering a *No, thank you*
which is buried by her *Don't give him anything*
but skim milk. My mother noisily stands, mentions arthritis

and moves, *I need a nap,* to their bedroom. I notice
the bent of her back, the small span of her steps—
she walks like an old woman, and I avert my eyes, flee

to their refrigerator—its white door spotted by brown moles,
bereft of anything that I could possibly desire—
to escape a contemplation of my parents' mortality.

From *Menage a Trois With the 21st Century*,
2004

Venus Rising For The First Time in the 21st Century

To see is this other torture, atoned for
in the pain of being seen
—from "Spokes" by Paul Auster

You want to see
her seeing
herself. You want

her seeing
her wanting
you behind the wave

foaming
when you become
the sea seeing

her eyes form
(above a body you
dreamt into salt water)

to see you
through strands
of dark seaweed

you see as her wet
hair rising from the sea
you become to see

her peeking from behind
hair of ink you want
to part from her breasts

you have felt
without seeing
yet (oh yet!)

to commence
a vision you
have shared with her

in her (lurking unknowingly)
through her
seeing you

as the sea
seeing her float
within your arms

trustingly as
she cannot swim
and your currents run deep

as deep as
the desire to be seen
she once forgot behind

a habit of hiding
until she saw you
seeing her

see(d)ing you
sea-ing her
seeing you

elicit pain
(the demanded pain!)
for surfacing the dark

fleshed creature
once hiding
in a sea's dim depths

towards a sun
in whose light
scars reveal themselves

to be healed
when you foam
upon seeing her form

seeing you sea
-ing her not drown
even as you deepen

your vision
's penetration to see
what others could not

behind her breasts
and thighs
now rising from the sea

towards the sun
so you can see
even more clearly

to see why you
foamed at the thought
of her form

returning to your
sea of seeing
whose fortitude

demands
nothing less than
the noonday sun as your lamp

Enheduanna #20

Vivo sin vivir en mi
"I live without inhabiting myself"
—**St. John of the Cross**

As you fall asleep
in my skin
will you dream?

Will you want
you or want
to change?

As you fall asleep
in my skin
how will I forget

and remember
you wanting
you in my skin?

Will you bring the scent
of red roses
I left behind

in New York City alleyways
(or has that season yet to pass)?
In my eyes

will you see
Baudelaire's infinity
he defined as the "sky"

you witness repeatedly
on and in any painting
marked by blue sapphire, lapis

lazuli, indigo, turquoise...sky...?
Will you fall into me
on a chair whose expanse

is a newly-birthed planet's?
Whose territory we shall explore
with you in my skin?

Will you articulate back
to me to teach me
the vocabulary I lose as I speak it?

Text with surfaces burnished
to shimmer
like certain elements you admire:

a beaded curtain, wet tile,
sea glass scattered on a wooden floor,
enamel on aluminum paintings?

Text whose materiality
gleams forth "Beauty"
as abstraction

while remaining palpably
fraught with meaning—
words like *Purity, Smoke, Thrall,*

Shield, Brush, Mote, Sheen...
"which is to say,"
letters that both signify

and are signified
to comprise *The Encyclopedia
of the Om*?

As you move into and in
my skin, will you remember
the ruby of a virgin moon

I once invoked
while you envied the pieces
of chocolate melting against my tongue?

And the milk complexion
of this same orb
as the moon ascends away from virginity?

And even as you shift
helplessly within me
will you only want to plunge deeper

into my skin you long now
to spread on a beach
crimsoned from leaves loosened by flame trees?

Where you then can taste
on my skin
the color of "sky and water"?

As you fall asleep
in my skin
will you dream of nuns

lifting black skirts
as they tease
the edge of a swiftly-traveling wave?

Will you pause in my skin
to look into my eyes
relishing there the plea you see

transform itself into
the eerie yellow light
photographed within the emerald

eyes of a sadhu
and know you are witnessing
Ecstasy—its path, fulfillment

and fulfillment into yet another path…?
Will you recall my memory
of the sadhu's naked figure

melding with the tanned face
of a sandstone cliff
as you watch and relish

my skin performing
what you are thinking
that I am thinking

until you begin to hear
a long-haired yogi breathe
over a class of bowed acolytes,

"Bless yourself, bless all beings,
bless yourself again"?
As you fall into my skin

will you see the white light
bathing the yogi's inner eye,
the same radiance I described

to you
while still courting
you to fall asleep

in my skin?
As I keep opening up
to your dream

will you hear all
of the portraits ever painted
by a man's gaze

of women immortalized
amidst (coiled with) desire
shift within their frames

as if they also feel you
falling asleep in their skin?
As if they wish to break

apart their gilded constraints?
Will my hands part
silk, then thighs,

to reveal a ziggurat, "Y*O*U,"
a tear, a dragonfly, a stag?
Once, as your sweat

becomes balm
for my lips
parched by the exertions

you compel from this flesh
containing your
wakeful sleep,

will you recall stumbling
across a girl's startled face
in a museum (infamous for a cheeky

ghost wandering through hallways
in search of a painting
written about but never made)

and feel my presence
though I was not that girl?
"If you recall," she wore

"holey" jeans and cobalt hair
that cast your mouth
into a gentle smile.

I have memorized this girl's tale
for its location in a city
you once shared with me

in the same time zone,
a period both our memories failed
to grasp so that I may write

this Poem
whose reality is the Ideal
for you in me

as you fall
into a sleep whose embrace
you desire to defer

as you fear how slumber may cause
you to forget you in my skin.
All this and still—oh still!—

I keep opening up
to you, to you falling asleep
in my skin!

And now you begin to taste
each undulation of my body
as "a molten mix of starfruit,

honey and pineapples"
while the air, too, begins
to become physical

by taking on the tinge
of fire, rose, ruby,
sunset, dawn, sunset ...

Perhaps you wish to pause again
briefly
to tease yourself along my damp nape

as I only want you
to keep falling, falling
asleep in my skin

though you cannot attain
such sleep. As you remain thrashing
in this place called "sweet insomnia"

(where I up poker stakes
against Artaud, Rimbaud, Baudelaire
and countless others making up "Anonymous")

my hair and its perfume
of musk your sweat
places there

also evoke in you in my skin
the first time I approached you
as "the blur of a cheek

shyly turning away,
hair covering eyes
and a murmured whisper."

What I whispered
was not pointless
but not the point

which is your desire
to fall asleep in my skin
and feel my tongue

share the taste of all colors
existing in this universe
glorious with multiplicities

whose possibilities include
a double rainbow
that connected dandelion clouds

over St. Helena's vines
hanging low with ripe purple fruit
while hungry ravens circled overhead.

The curving prisms revealed
where cauldrons of gold
lit up the depths of a pond

embedded as a bead of azure
into earth,
just as you now are deep

-ly embedded in my skin.
So deep you even begin
to hear a tango

danced by a silver-haired lady
sheathed in black velvet
as you feed me spicy chorizo

sausages, crisp-skinned and blood
-stuffed morcillas studded with raisins,
crusty sweetbreads and tender kidneys

in a feast that will leave you and me
ravaged but even more ravenous
for each other's flesh.

As you fall
asleep
in my skin

I shall stoke up the fire
deepening the furrow on your brow
by offering the gesture women

have made for centuries
to those they wish to please:
the pouring of your wine

into a goblet
as heavy as the armor
I released upon feeling

your hunger to fall
into my skin.
My hand on a decanter

spills "libations" (becomes "Biblical," no less!)
to prepare for your sleep
in my skin (but only after other…actions).

I recognize your longing
for my hand
's approach for your pleasure

after you memorized that same gesture
I saw immortalized
as oil on canvas across a table

set in damask, crystal, silver,
porcelain, a candle's flame
a low bowl spilling forth vermilion blooms….

Deeper still you fall
into my skin
to bring us both to Tuscany

where your fingers linger
on certain spots of my flesh
normally hidden from the world

until I gasp and rear up
from linen named "Solace"
edged in a series of thin stripes

whose colors someone adeptly
labeled celery, parchment, creme brulee,
persimmon, blue sage, black pearl….

You anticipated my love
for the vocabulary of fabrics: how red
becomes claret, green becomes khaki

or caca d'oie, oranges become brick,
cinnamon or terra cotta. As you revel in
anonymity through my skin, you repeat this list

for you know I love any litany
of words whose shapes
your lips form against my skin.

Even more, I urge you in, in,
in-to my skin
to bring you back

to my childhood
farm where I browned
a younger version

of these legs
(you now nibble for you're a tease)
by playing with freshly-plucked tobacco leaves.

This same memory surfaced
while I was still spinning
fairy tales to lure you

into falling asleep in my skin,
like a story about a cigar shoppe
on Sixth Avenue with another

list which, simply by making my lips
move, reminded me of you:
Macamundo, Push, Hoyo de Monterrey,

Cohiba Partagas, Excalibur, Davidoff,
Zino. With you in my skin, I now dance
with your tongue as I promise

I shall stand before you someday
somewhere in Gevrey-Chambertin
releasing from my waist a voluminous skirt

whose ribbons you shall admire
for shimmering like sunlit rivers.
The images from these stories,

and more (for there is always more
between us), such as steel skyscrapers
piercing fat, grey clouds, or a tapestry

called "Marly" from whose greenery bursts
small red berries like blood drops
spool through your mind

as you fall asleep
in my skin
where, yes, you dream

and dream and dream
until you recall even a painting of deer
I once confused for mules

because, once, you mentioned an island
whose white heat surrounded you
falling asleep in my skin.

Where mules waited patiently
beneath the shade of olive trees
as you sculpted a milk puddle

on the floor from the translucent shift
whose lace strap you ripped
when it dared to halt your fall

into my skin. As Athena and Venus
battled for my fidelity ("as if I ever
would lapse to a binary").

And I remember Greece again
When you fall into my skin
elsewhere: a hotel room

dimmed by a palette of pearls
except for the rug bearing
Joseph's "many colors"

woven by long-dead boys
when only thin cloths protected their limbs
from a scorching sun. On this rug

smoothened to velvet
through centuries of downtrodden existence
you fall into my skin

but fail once more to sleep
as you feel me write a new poem
by licking and biting it into your skin.

A poem that sears
even as you heave
and plead, then demand: "Never...ever...stop...!"

You fall into my skin
through yet another occasion
by joining me in the company

of dark-suited men flinging silk ties
behind their shoulders
before their knives slice meat

again and again.
Since you are not asleep
in my skin, you hear a red-nosed

man howl from "La Traviata"
as our group banters in a room
whose walls of ancient teak

once formed an explorer's ship.
In my skin, you see the occasional seep
of blood on my plate and feel yourself

infiltrated by the future memory of animals
roasting on fires ablaze
beneath a night sky

where flames leap towards the stars,
where the shadows beneath your eyes
in my skin turn lavender, where even

the air feels primitive as hunters' rifles lean
against fallen logs. With you in my skin,
I shall pour into your glass the elements

of earth, leather, currants, gravel, tobacco,
oak, plums and voluptuous tears.
This meal unfolds itself as sheer opulence,

like the texture you feel from my skin,
velvet heating up beneath your roving palms
until I burn up everything

that was me before you fell
into my skin. Until you are the only one
filling me. And you fill me

also with Merleau-Ponty's
"syrupy and shimmering element,"
this "radiation of the visible"

sought by painters
"beneath the words
depth, space and colour."

You fall so deeply, so deeply
into my skin you begin
to recover all the memories

I've forgotten, such as Germany.
Where I peered at rainy Vilseck
between the huge biceps

of red-cheeked farmers in overalls
downing stein after stein
of gleaming amber beer. Such as Kauai

where my helicopter plunged
almost as deeply as you are falling
into my skin. Plummeted along

a 90-degree line mirrored by the groove
of a thin waterfall that foretold
the same straight line you,

in my skin, now trace with a nerve
-wracked but determined finger
beginning its caress from the furrow

deepening on your brow
before falling on down, down,
down...your will moving my hand

to the destination where you want
yourself in my skin to land.
And as I continue to do your bidding

because you are in my skin
(though I would enact your wishes
even if you had not yet began

to fall into my skin
for Beauty's expanse
also includes a "sense of dislocation")

you uncover a secret
involving the shadow of a cross
spilling against a 19th century

Shahsavan carpeting a granite floor.
Though this is not the place to say more
about that particular story

whose material includes the nuance
of teal, the fabric of chintz and the incongruity
of cabbage roses encasing arm chairs

you will hear that tale someday
and think no less of me
for you will have been in my skin

sufficiently by then to understand
how someone motivated by
"Never Enough"

was simply struggling (like 80-year-old Henry Moore)
to manage "the constant
breathing moments of a dedicated life."

And as you continue falling
now into the final stages
before we exhaust ourselves

into a sleep that still fails
to be deep enough to still your hands
from moving across skin

to please you, that still
fails to be deep enough to still
my lashes from fluttering

over each additional inch
measured out by your journey
of you in my skin, we begin to see

together the eye-narrowing glimmer of wind
shifting along an ocean's silver surface,
the curl of a leaf dropping

on a different continent, pencil-thin
smoke rising behind ten thousand mountains.
Of course, we spot the "hole"

defined by sailors as "no wind."
You fall so deeply into my skin
we fling ourselves to topple

the barrier into a parallel universe
where you and I no longer need
to imagine each other. Where you and I

unlock our fate from the aftermath
of missing each other in a city
we once shared for decades.

You fall so deeply into my skin
you detoxify me
from my addiction to a cloudy mirror

and release me into the "necessary
blindness" of the night
required for my hands to flail

about so widely that they finally
encounter you now falling
asleep in my skin

where, yes, you dream
me dreaming we are not dreaming
as you fall deeply into my skin.

Where, yes, you want
you as you find you
in my skin.

Where you have fallen
so deeply
when you awake in my skin

I shall plead, "Stay…"
Please stay:
"Forget memory"

Please stay.
Please return as you in me
to a time before memory.

Before the "beginning"
erroneously defined in books
long since relegated to dust.

Before the beginning,
before you became you
and I became I,

you were in my skin
as I was in yours.
But the beginning arrived

with the *Word*
that separated
"You" from "I."

Now, with your homecoming
into my skin
I plead, "Please stay…"

I feel feathers falling
from angels ripping off halos
to peek through Heaven's widening rip

as I plead:
"Forget memory.
Please stay…"

And you
And you
And you

cease being careful,
obviate your history of reticence,
obviate memory

"and, and, *And!*"
declare the death
of the she-wolf Chicheface

whose stomach was so delicate
she only could eat
"virtuous women," a concept

you dismiss
for you in my skin
accept Poetry's demands

to privilege risk,
compelling you now to raise
a finger to place against my lips

to silence me
(finally!)
so that my eyes can hear you

Speak—
Stay—
Speak—

Speak
The Word
A E I O U

A A A
E E E
I I I

I I I
O O O
U U You...

From *I Take Thee, English,*
For My Beloved, 2005

Tercets From The Book of Revelation
—after Rupert Thomson's "The Book of Revelation"

(i)
How does the air
come to pulse
like a muscle

As if your scent
lingers
before your arrival

How does the night
come to press
and smother

As if fresh wounds
must accompany
revelations

Church bells ring
over a dark street
to fracture glass

Or was it a childhood
memory evoking
how light becomes distant

A fine, silvery mist
descends
on a wall, a city

You reach me
by penetrating past
a train's smoke and whistle

Damp hair clings
to the nape
of your neck

How can the cause
for an absence
lose relevance

How many stories
do we deny
to obviate recitation

How do we pretend
no boats mutter
along the salted, wet dock

How did I give up
your child
for an imagined affair

A pine forest
breathes for me
behind an empty house

He looked happy
before meeting
a burglar's intimacy

You can reach me
by noticing how trees
shiver by the edge of a road

How a sun
flattens the water
of a grey canal

How does release
from what you love
become "unequivocal freedom"

Sunglasses hang
against her breastbone
from a silver chain

No limits surround
the purple sheen
to Montenegro lilies

Afterwards
why do you never
hold me

How do I find
the necessary vein
I must mine

To determine
the difference between
coincidence and grace

(ii)
How does one see
significance
in brackets studding a wall

Or be claimed
through a stranger's
tattoo

"I want to see you
again to know
I was not dreaming"

A church, a girl, a cloud,
a fragmented tune—of what
are they coordinates

Children cluster
within a tree's branches
like birds, fruit, pollen

A shirt cuff
so white
it forms an independent image

It has never been
my desire for men
to take second place

I always wake
before the alarm clock
begins to irradiate

A man weeps tonight
with the father
of a schizophrenic son

How does one offend
by innocently asking
"Are you happy?"

In Zanzibar
fruit bats
fragment a room's dimness

Upon meeting, you
knew to suggest
"Alchemy needs your silence"

Wildflowers override
the trenches
of a battlefield

There are days when
the world's kindness
forgives pastis imbibed at zinc bars

A man blows a saxophone
until the moon
turns to butter

To approximate immortality
through the art
of doing nothing

Burying stories
I cannot reveal
within those I can

Her hair offers
the scent of firecrackers
reaching for the Milky Way

"Put it in
me now,"
she whispers

When he wants
to protect me
he holds my wrist

The air pulses
like a muscle
attentive and fraught

Adjectives From The Last Time They Met

How do bellboys learn
to accept the most impoverished suitcase
as if it cossets a woman's auriferous secret

A mahogany table gleams
with the glimmer of unshed tears
but some postlude always dissipates

the vespertine effect of opulence:
in this case, deodorizing perfume—
cloying despite wide corridors of Persian carpets

She sits for a moment
in her wet, hors de combat raincoat
eyes closed, wishing

she had talent for deep breathing
for integral yoga. Beyond the Grand Guignol window
twin skyscrapers frame a gray lake

In a different year, she had witnessed a wall
melt behind Max Gimblett's "Hibiscus Coast (2001)"
She is haunted by this Roman a clef

painting of four golden circles
whose intersections transform
a flower into an archetype—a heart's caparison

How to convince desk clerks
confusion is a matter of philippic physics:
"too little time for too much to think"

A gilded mirror takes in
with much complacency (a lack of taphophobia)
the All-ness of the damask-covered, King-sized bed

From the street, 32 floors below
a husband and wife enact a postmodern hastilude
despite their shared feeling of chthonic deja vu

How to make impresario earrings
of pink, dangling lucite
erase chagrin from her shoulders

when next she approaches
an adamantine podium embossed
with an insurance company's logo

Dusk shall offer hors d'oeuvres
of a "conventional nature" (their colors scumbled on brass trays)
she anticipates without acrimony

A woman with emerald eyes
shall display feral teeth
between collagen-injected lips in sternutation

A man with a huge belly
billowing a shirt so white it blinds
shall monopolize the guacamole amidst argy-bargy

She shall try to butter a cracker
with eldritch, blue-veined cheese
But the sesame-dotted wafer shall break

disintegrating between her fingers
like a lost score with a furtive history
whose notes she is anguishing to recall, then obviate

She shall hover over a bowl
of fruit with nictitating skins, only to
balk at sensing grapes browning

along their edges. As she shudders
from hearing cream curdle
within its xanthic, porcelain pitcher

she shall see a former lover
for the first time in two decades—
his hands shall be pale and cyanic

like winter, soft like
his cartographer's tones as he addressed
her during the first year

of a sweet, awkward courtship
when her belly was still telegenic
and nipples demure

"Middle age," he shall say
"is lovely on you"
She shall lower already circumspect eyelids

from a panic on the brink
of becoming more than mild
She shall hear invisible bees caught in a trammel

Later, they shall share salmon
with black grill marks
made affable by cucumber salad

He shall query hesitantly, sensitively
about children she has never birthed
Her breath shall sear her chest

"Did you ever keep our letters?"
he shall ask while scrambling for a nugatory subject
In response, she shall feel utterly spilled

A loud diner at the next table
shall catalogue a rebus of atrocities
witnessed by the sky over Rwanda

Once, for no obvious reason, she shall
yen for gold-rimmed china
and thick crystal she has never accepted

wrapped in gilded paper, bound by silver ribbons,
during an affair involving a taffeta gown, veil
and rented majordomo. Certain objects

are diminished when not received as gifts
They shall utter things (perhaps bipartisan;
perhaps none even shall be banal)

Still, one of them shall proclaim ex cathedra
"Farewell" through an abrupt concession:
Time does not help

How next shall an ineffable conversation unfold
when dessert must yet be served
then a speech heard from an honored guest

Another couple in the room
shall persist in a derring do quarrel, both knowing
silence is too liminal to beget victory

Before the night shall end everyone's gravamens
with centerfold lilies barely
holding on to lavender complexions

a woman shall hiss in capitulation
at a man she has just met
"Don't fuck with me"

and feel good for the first time
that year. As if she survived
the unsolved murder of her only child

After an honored guest's speech
that they shall hear as
the pellucid sound of mating fireflies

they once shared together
in a time involving air scented
with frangipani, now relegated to their dreams

they shall discover themselves acquiescent
in the woman's hotel room
The bed shall be encased in cashmere

One shall become Magdalene
who shall wash feet
before drying it with hair

They shall remember
another day with a fulgent sky
when her slip was damp with the sea

and he described the zoomorphic hour
"as salt, as salt"
while she curled her palms into fists

However it shall end
its pachydermic legacy shall be the sense
of a miracle that occurred

but so swiftly and tenderly
compassion shall always be a required
precedent to its auriferous memory

Mudra

—after "Tantric Suite" by Rod Paras-Perez

To kiss the moon
Suspended
Between the soles of her feet

She must become
The essence
Of flexibility

By sitting cross-legged
On the floor
And lowering her back

To form a circle
By dropping her brow
Between her knees

Not like a snake
Swallowing
Its tail

Like compassion
Flexing its muscles
To accept everything, everything, *everything*

For Charles Henri Ford

The glowworm
turns professorial
when stars hide

A white azalea
quiets the shade
into a girl

The girl loves marble
enough to freeze
into a swoon

While ascending from trellis jail
the jasmine's skin
comes to mirror the sky

From a factory
questionable grit escapes
within the cover of gray haze

You want to live
You live to want
As if to anguish is to feel

Tongue the cracks
to glue together
fragments of a stolen sun

Revel
in the claw marks
forking a cheek

Oh, Poet
preening at the labyrinth—
unlatch that gate

You, there
with blue veins
crackling transparent membrane

From *Post Bling Bling*, 2005

Vain Terse-et

V
A
N
I
T
Y

FAIR

V
A
N
I
T
Y

FAR

V
A
N
I
T
Y

AIR

Be Yourself At Home

Topless
    Wet
        White

at
The Mandalay Bay
Las Vegas

"Paloma's Groove"

Accessories from $95 to $275—
Paloma Picasso
    @ Tiffany.com

From *The Secret Lives of Punctuations, Vol. I,*
2006

Parenthetical Tercets

('twas the first time
she sewed for bit-
maps)

(regret a kingdom
with unknown
borders)

(is it possible
for a decade to
weep?)

(oh, the
awkwardness of
trust!)

(but a tobacco hiccup
enhances the
pinprick's wake)

From *Dredging For Atlantis*, 2006

Burning Pulpit

Could our two miseries
copulate
into one opulent being?

Men simplify
then slink back
to antediluvian burrows

Baby priests
turn away
to cast profiles forsworn to Donatello

But she is clutching lilac print
within a shadow burning away
salvation's seedlings

Funny Brass

Dawn
(like my puppy)
penetrates eyelash drapes

Man becomes
Woman
by losing aloofness

"Monotone"
transforms to
"Moonstone"

Go forth
and prettily
miscalculate

From *The Light Sang As It Left Your Eyes:*
Our Autobiography, 2007

Ifugao Red

A collaboration by Nick Carbo and Eileen Tabios

Wings flare. Hawk soars
as if the sky is Ifugao red
and her wrists shake

with seven silver bracelets, each
dangling a stone etched with
memories formed as feathers,

teardrops, arrowheads. The sound
of her grandmother crushing
gabi leaves for a spell

fills the room. The window persists
with its lack of your face
supplanting the pumice stones

during the monsoon season
in Pampanga. After tasting
salt through her tears

why did you open your pores
to the temptress' curved copper
tongue? Does the witch paint

heavy verbs on your thighs? Boulders
like "ravage," "pillage," "ransack"
or "despoiled"? Peel off their signs

for sweetness: her damp eyes walking
to the front mahogany door
to answer your wing beats

discerned through the breeze.
To arrive home is to release your
armor, dropping it on ancient terrazzo.

"Find" is a Verb

A collaboration by Nick Carbo and Eileen Tabios

Bowdlerized books of history—
those pages where she flamed
aghast at marmalade and toast

-colored fricative verbs. Instead
belly bulged from blackened goat
with privilege ascribed to charred skin

the pensive prepuce would not
touch. Allow pastiche, she cooed.
"To collage is to include the world."

"Poetry Criticism"
—for Paul Auster, and after his Collected Poems

1.
What if
        all along
the interior was stone?

All along
        what if
stone defined the absence of void?

Do poems cancel
        foolishness
from questions?

If not, does not the stone palm
        crack—
the pieces never to be caught?

2.
Nearly blinded me,
        this stone
splinter released by sun.

Blood on fingers
        after brushing
cheek's glimmer of bone.

Pain a most
        effective tool
for obviating abstraction(s).

Dear Stranger,
        After all this time
my lips shall memorize yours

Literally.

Copper Rain
(after Christian Hawkey's "A Coppery Rain Slashes Through It")

and then the kiss
and then the greeting
"swollen underground with rain"

whisper
song
stairway

Where Everything Is Clear

(after Christian Hawkey's "Up Here in the Rafters Everything Is Clear")

left with a stare watching itself
a poem in a forest
covered deeply by ancient moss

its legacy a stone toe
red paint long faded
(though it lingers as memory)

somewhere, a woman
shrouds herself in white linen
a poem invisible but transparent

Storm Trooper

(after Christian Hawkey's "Since Judgment Is Also A Storm")

Clouds a moving prop
fail to soften
the edges of dark architecture

Wet bark
dissolving into itself—
what remains…

You always played it safe
But don't you see
how nothing is truly measurable…

Nerves Say

(after Christian Hawkey's "The Nervous Man in a Four-Dollar Room")

slamming doors
light switch lit
blindfold tossed away

clearing stomach
from embers
slipped through ears

the ear only a hole
for burning stones
tossed by a cruel world

After A Departure
(after Christian Hawkey's "Note Left Behind on a Table")

a mirrored face
only partially owned
by its reflection

an incomplete suicide note
a trompe l'oeil painting slip-
ping to surrealism

fishes flying overhead
always wide-eyed
always breathless, unbelieving

a long-haired woman exists
but outside the frame
as has been reality for centuries now…

Copper Rain Redux

and then the kiss
and then the greeting
"swollen underground with rain"

whisper
    song
        stairway

stairway
    singing
        whisper

whisper
    singing
        stairway

stairway
    whispering
        song

From *Footnotes to Algebra:*
Uncollected Poems 1995-2009, 2009

The Rebel's Son

Skinny. Toys of twigs, cracked stones,
two matchboxes cradling spiders,
an earthworm in a tin can. Ignored

by neighbors fussing over mother fussing
over father's impending arrival.
Hums to himself as women weep

over their best bowls and platters
created by foregoing
yesterdays' meals. What they offer

is meager: also more than generous.
Skinny. Approaches the table
—hears a grumble begin beneath his ribs

at the sight of more food than his home
has ever contained at any one moment in time.
But he waits patiently for father's return:

it will be the first time his father
will not pass through the door on his own feet.
He will arrive a hero borne

unbegrudgingly on bony shoulders—
a hero contained by a wooden container
mother described with an alien word: coffin.

An eternity earlier, father placed calloused palms
on each of Skinny's cheeks. Father said, "I must go
to feed your body, your spirit, my spirit."

Hums to hide his question to the earthworm,
"Didn't father know I would rather not eat
than have him live forever in that box?"

78

An eternity later, (still) Skinny marvels still
at the definition of *dictatorship*—
people eating their fill only at funerals.

Montana: A Novel

This
is the worst
country for

extremes.
Fortunately, I love
weather's ~~swiftly~~ cruel

changes.
They make me
feel this

country
isn't just flat
placid landscape—

that
it's as violent
as dark

Doone
country or any
wild Cornish

coast
you read about
in English

novels.
I feel you
listening, *listening*…

breathing
scent of black
earth dampening…

Ellen: Chapter 2

We watched
the storm arrive
steel-like

against yellow-gray
sky. We could
see

the first
drops hit, whacking
forth

a sound
like the scattering
of

broken beads
to look like
rock

salt pockmarking
long-suffering ground. Tomorrow
farmers

will swap
stories of hailstones
bigger

than any
from memory. We
watched

them smash
the nasturtiums I
watered

all summer
with dishwater. But
then

I realized
sitting there where
hailstones

hit my
shoes and bounced
back

down the
steps: I did
not

care what
the cracking heaven
ruined.

Tears slid
as we watched
but

I mourned
mostly that I
did

not care
what will become
shattered.

I realized
I had stopped
waiting

for the
storm to stop.
One

foot kicked
back at one
hailstone

but I
realized I no
longer

waited for
the storm to
cease

and desist.

Girl Singing:

To-Day

Girl singing. Day. You watching

and longing. Skirt flaring. Time
stops: smooth limbs flirting
with sunlight. You watching. Day.

Yellow barrette loosens. Hair
floats. Unfolds. Swirls like
what I see when I think of infant

typhoons. Girl singing. Glee:
skirt flies to reveal knees
puckered for your kisses. Day. You

watching, breath forgotten. You
long. Oh, how you long for this
moment never to cease! Like

a cold winter afternoon on Madison
Avenue. When you felt replete
with joy: despite the chill, the sky—

the sky!—a sunlit ceiling of blue.
Seamless. Girl singing. Day. You
feel now that same Mediterranean sun

warming the pavement before your
limping feet. You feel the sun
smiling. Girl singing. Day. Heaven

nearer than a breath away.

Girl Singing:

Brubeck Notes

Girl singing. Day. Dave Brubeck

on stage. White linen blazer. White
hair. Regaling the audience with a tale.
Fireflies dancing in his eyes.

His wife was clearing the sun porch for visitors:
"children, grand-children and great-grandchildren"—
the latter proclaimed with utmost pride!

Girl singing. Day. "We needed all
the beds and all the floor space
we could muster," proclaimed *The Father*

of West Coast Cool. Mrs. Brubeck
stumbled across an old manuscript,
brought it to him and asked, "What

do you think this is?" He scanned
the faded notes, played them on the piano
then robustly proclaimed with glee:

"I don't know what it is but it's damn
good." Mr. Brubeck decided to finish
the old tune. Girl singing. Day.

As his wife continued to clear the porch
she found the song's second half
from years ago. But Mr. Brubeck preferred

his new conclusion. To everyone's delight,
his choice was proven right when
he and his trio performed "The Time of Our

Madness"—Randy Jones on drums, Jack
Six on string bass, Bobby Militello on saxophone
and Girl singing. Day. Sometimes, the perfect

pitch needs time. Like bottles of champagne
rotated in their racks, inch by inch
meticulously for months. Or cabernet settling

in oak barrels buried in underground caves.
Like basting Thanksgiving turkey for twelve
hours straight. Time passing. Girl singing.

Day. Like Mr. Brubeck's turn to music
only after studying pre-med to heal cattle
as a vet. Oh! These long, long days for

Heaven nearer than a breath away.

Girl Singing:

A True Story
—Villa Montalvo, September 11, 1999

Girl singing. Day. Breath

suspended as you watch me run.
Curve my footsteps to mirror the hill.
Face lifts to see your cautious

watch. You peer behind
the falling leaves of ancient pines.
Girl singing. Day. I slow my pace

to recall a fairy tale: a boy
and a bear who stumble upon
each other. In a forest like this

moment with you and me.
His innocence untested, the boy runs
toward the bear. Boy ecstatic

with glee. Girl singing. Day.
The big bear backed off,
teeth and paws clambering away.

"You" are three large deer
and I but one mortal. One girl
singing. One day. I never knew

a deer could grow so huge-ly!
I quicken my footsteps as you
watch me sing. Day. A few more

feet then, simultaneously, your tableaux
leaps down the hill. Leaves flutter.
Butterflies rise. Girl singing. Day. I

rise like Mama's bread. Like Aphrodite
fresh from a god's sundered brow.
Follow the curve up this Montalvo hill.

Round the gravel path towards a villa
glinting beneath blue sky. Girl singing.
Day. A bride at the top of white marble

steps. White silk gown. Gauzy white
veil. A cascade of roses from pale hands.
Eyes looking fearlessly at the sun.

Honey blossom air. The goddess
smiles. It's my 39th birthday today.
Girl singing. Day. Heaven

nearer than a breath away…

Girl Singing:

39

Girl singing. Day. When "I"

is a Verb, the leaf beyond
my bedroom window becomes
a universe for contemplation

rather than a mere fragment
at the mercy of a faint breeze.
"I" have strolled unthinkingly

through forest paths and supermarket
parking lots, in both cases halted
by the unexpected desire to cherish

the coiling orange peel, the mesh of
(the fortune in?) tea leaves
layering a chipped porcelain cup,

the sinking nub of a pencil's eraser—
all have nourished with a generosity
belied by the spent gestures to which

they have come to rest. Girl singing.
Day. Once, I longed to visit Egypt
whose people learned how to measure

light—thus, the larger inheritance
they have bequeathed to you and me:
our glorious planet is a village

for it is round! Girl singing. Day.
For a globe enables my "I" to return
always to you no matter how far I stray.

Girl singing. Day. And my friend Mr. Bean
is also correct about the charms of "3"
and "9"—both open, flirtatious,

loopily and exuberantly depicting
coupling curves. Girl singing. Day.
In such small details lie Heaven

nearer than a breath away.

Girl Singing:

Unity

Girl singing. Day. *La luna naranja.*

A crimson moon. Lit by the longest
wave light from the spectrum of the sun
sinking beneath the gold-

rimmed curve of the horizon.
Girl singing. Day. Sun
falls, moon rises—a difference

cast only from perspective. An
outlook ever shifting, always in
flux. Like the natives in Nepal,

diminutive in stature but overwhelming
through expansive smiles. Girl singing.
Day. Nepal—where I looked down

to see up: the Himalayas robustly dancing
with gods' puppets formed
from loose-limbed clouds. Ancient

mountains quivering like 500-pound
Sumo wrestlers. Girl singing. Day.
Moon reaches for the stars. Whitens

as its ascent receives the blessing
of the sun's full spectrum. Mother-
of-pearl face. A calmness after

a sanguine birth. A Taoist Master
dribbling white whiskers holds moonlight
on open palm. Strong breathing

evoking the sun's spirit: hidden but
never diminished. Girl singing. Day.
Heaven present in the smallest leaf.

Heaven nearer than a breath away.

Girl Singing:

The Secret Life of an Angel

Girl singing. Day. The old man

of winter reaches for immortality
with a lengthening shadow
despite my skipping away.

Girl singing! I insist. Day!
I chant like the *Babaylan* I will
become to keep the clouds

from dimming the sun, from
milking the sky of its cobalt
gaze. He has worn many

disguises, and I have let him:
the original angel who fell
and fell. "It's a glorious ride,"

he has whispered as part of his
spell. "This is a game of poker
I have lost, but no longer wish

to play," I reply. Girl singing.
Day. I insist and proclaim:
"You cannot scoff, my secret

demon. For I played with high
stakes while you only watched."
Girl singing. Day. I risked

everything while you hedged
so I could sing notes
only virgin boys can muster,

only fearful dogs can hear.
I lost myself in the "valley
of evil" but my wings unfurled

to make me rise. Unlike your
wings, mine did not betray—
unfurling as I changed my mind

for Heaven nearer than a breath away.

Girl Singing:

Forgiveness

Girl singing. Day. It occurs to me

I have loved well despite fire
burning the white gown
mother once knelt to hem

for me. I have loved well
despite the stake to which you
tied my limbs. Warriors led by

generals out of retirement
rounded curves recklessly
to rescue me. Girl singing.

Day. Before a young soldier
freed me—his scent of milk
my fresh air—I had breathed

in your sorrow. Day. I forgive:
may you never know cold
ashes and burlap. May you never

feel tar and black feathers. May
you know what I saw through
flames: a star leaving night

to sunder cerulean sky and hover
as hope. Girl singing. Day.
Stallions soared over moats

and blade-tipped barricades
by following the light
of the star that sundered night.

Girl singing. Day. May you
know rebirth through a second
chance. May you live in Heaven

nearer than a breath away.

Girl Singing:

Dearest Nelson,

—*after* A TRANSATLANTIC LOVE AFFAIR: Letters to Nelson Algren
by Simone De Beauvoir

Saturday, 12th July 1947

Girl singing. Day. Simone visits

Porto Vecchio. Lobster at noon. Dinner,
too. "A fine little village" despite a
"dirty little inn." Half-naked girls

on walls—"all kinds with black or
red hair." But then "a nice little
tortoise walking on the bed, and

everywhere." Girl singing. Day.
Dusk brings a "whole village, lighted
with candles." Young and old listen

"in a very intense way" to a dark-
haired communist girl explain
"what is fascism." Simone confides

"I do not like the CP, but
I liked the people trying so hard
to learn something about the big world."

Girl singing again the following Day
despite bus delays, a "half-dressed"
driver and rushing down "narrow

winding roads."
        "Everybody laughing and laughing
        and nobody caring for lost time."

The joy of arriving at some "poor inn"
where peasants eat "bad oily soup"
and drink red wine. Girl singing.

The next Day: the bus is halted,
then surrounded, by "a lot of little
partridges"! Simone clapping hands

with glee! "Everybody being crazy."
Then an evening gunshot that turns
everyone "mad with excitement."

Only to be "very disappointed for
nobody was killed." No chastising
sense of irony. "I like the way they

enjoy life"! Girl singing. I like
the way they "make excitement"!
Day. Later, in the water, Simone

can barely swim, only moves a little:
"Yet I like it very much." Oh,
"Nelson, my love." "My own

Nelson." "Mon bien-aime." I
describe the "fine country of
Corsica" so that I share this Heaven

across an ocean, but a breath away.

Girl Singing:

Plant Latin

Girl singing. Day. *Osmanthus*

Fragrans peering through polka dots
and lace. *Prunus Laurocerasus*
standing tall and proper. Then

Gieijera Parviflora picnicking by
mushroom caps without ants on
the lawn. Girl singing. Day.

Salvia Leucantha timidly turns
a brick corner. *Callistemon
Cupressifolius* insists he's not—

oh, he's not!—short. *Callistemon
Phenicus 'Prostrata'* always
fiery, never prostate. Girl

singing. Day. *Pyracantha
Coccinea* touting fire deep within
her cornucopia. *Prunus Cerasifera*

Cultivar damming violet tears.
Trachycarpus Fortunei blowing
dandelions off their feet. *Plum-*

bago Auriculata a felt cloak,
a felt beret. Girl singing. Day.
Acer Buergerianum no longer

a weapon, but an elegant maple.
Doryanthes Palmeri no longer
a weapon, just the shyest

of lilies. Girl singing strangely.
But it remains Day. Silly girl
singing for heaven hovers

nearer than a breath away.

Girl Singing:

Infinity's Fragment

An acorn nudges me
I feel Your hand
lift up my face

> *Girl singing. Day…*

Poetics (#1)

What we wanted
to do
to be

was what we were helpless
against doing
against being

ROI

With this book
I best
the best of Wall Street

II. HAY(NA)KU

a form of integration and conjunction

—Karla Kelsey

Some Poets on the Hay(na)ku

I find the word-based formal constraint of hay(na)ku (as opposed to a syllable or metrical foot based constraint) leads to poems that are in many ways more natural, and that, in particular, the 1-2-3 structure is a pattern that comes up continually in the course of the daily. Poetry lives and breathes in the daily, and hay(na)ku has the ability to capture profound and delightful pieces that might otherwise be missed.

—Dan Waber

The arbitrariness of word count would seem to leave things wide open for content, syllabic play, and a variety of languages—at least with the hay(na)ku (rather than, say, the haiku). And because of this, I think the hay(na)ku is a good (if challenging) container for conceptual writing. It's a very "light" form, structurally; one doesn't feel burdened by it.

—Jean Vengua

The diasporic nature of the hay(na)ku attracted me from the very beginning because it allowed me to express myself in English without being a native speaker…. I feel the hay(na)ku is a form that grants a common space for poetic practice in different languages; a way of writing in English without completely obliterating one's "mother tongue." Instead of the conquest and influx that has defined English in relation to other "less powerful" languages, the hay(na)ku is open and flexible, an invitation to share different ways of thought and writing.

—Ernesto Priego

Watching the birth & evolution of a new form is fascinating. And, unlike flarf, which is a process, hay(na)ku is a form. But what kind of form is it? Poem or stanza? Again, I think the answer lies in looking at the quatrain, which is more stanza than finished work. That, ultimately, is what I think this first generation of hay(na)ku writers have created—not a poem, but a stanza, simple, supple, elegant, capable of considerable variation. That's quite an accomplishment.

—Ron Silliman

…an elegantly minimalist form (a bit like the tip of an Oulipian "snowball")

—Michael Leong

Why I love the hay(na)ku: Because of the zip & pop of it … the flame & spark of it. Like snapping a towel at someone you love.

—Aimee Nezhukumatathil

The hay(na)ku is fun to read and fun to write. I like beginning with one word. It puts everything into focus almost immediately. It's an extreme condensation that feels more natural in English (or Tagalog or French) than as an imitation of the Japanese model, if that makes sense. It's hard to write haiku without wind chimes and seasonal changes. The tradition is so infused with those things. It's nice having a new form that accomplishes the same goals but with more directness, more dexterity.

—John Olson

…a way of revealing…a "thinking" form—emotional as well as intellectual thinking. By allowing a lot of space on the page it keeps things tight and loose. Hay(na)ku creates or pushes certain syntactical structures, potentially disruptive through its arbitrariness. Forms aren't games, or just games—they are ways of paying attention.

—Jill Jones

Every word counts. That's hard to resist in The Age of Logorrhea. The form encourages paring, discourages padding. Lines shaped by word count rather than syllable engendering more rhythmic variety among poems and within the poem itself. Enjambment abound, bounds.

—Crag Hill

Hay(na)ku
flexibly tempered
to American speech

received sound pearls
fit (un)tutored
hearing.

—Sheila E. Murphy

The History of the Hay(na)ku

In 2000, I began a "Counting Journal" with the idea that counting would "be just another mechanism for me to understand my days." I intended to do so by counting everything countable within my daily life. That journal lasted for only five months because I could maintain its underlying obsession for only that long.

My Counting Journal was inspired, as this first entry explained on Sept. 20, 2000, by Ianthe Brautigan's *You Can't Catch Death—A Daughter's Memoir* which noted the character Cameron in her celebrated father Richard Brautigan's *The Hawkline Monster:* "Cameron was a counter. He vomited nineteen times to San Francisco. He liked to count everything."

I came to present excerpts from my Counting Journal on my first poetics blog, "WINEPOETICS" (http://winepoetics.blogspot.com). On my last counting-related blog entry, I wrote:

> *Rather than spend more days having you witness me gazing into that part of my navel where Brautigan's eyes are twinkling back, let me write a last Counting post. This one will feature snippets based on which page the journal opens to when I drop it on the floor.*
>
> *Drop Journal: Page opens onto 12/18/00. Bush secured Electoral College majority—271 votes—to become the U.S.' 43rd President. It was announced that Hillary Clinton received an $8.0 mio. advance for a memoir for her years in the White House. With Simon and Schuster. So much $ for gossip when one can't even find the more modest sum to publish a poetry book!*
>
> *Ugh. Close Journal. Drop Journal Again. Page opens onto 1/28/01: On plane returning to San Francisco, read Selected Letters of Jack Kerouac. P. 46—Kerouac says, "I think American haikus should never have more than 3 words in a line—e.g.*
>
> *Trees can't reach*
> *for a glass*
> *of water*

[I found Kerouac's thought sufficiently inspiring so that,] in
response, I am inaugurating the Filipino Haiku! Pinoy Poets:
Attention! I'll post if you send me some!: 3 lines each having one,
two, three words in order—e.g.

Trees
can't reach
for a glass

Enough Filipino (or "Pinoy") poets responded to my blog-post so that
I was able just two days later to introduce to the larger public a poetic
form I called the "Pinoy Haiku." Aptly, it was introduced on Philippine
Independence Day or June 12 of 2003.

Filipino poets responded with enthusiasm partly because, as Filipino-
American poet Michelle Bautista pointed out, the idea of one-two-three
"works with the Filipino nursery rhyme: *isa, dalawa, tatlo, ang tatay mo'y kalbo*
(pronounce phonetically to catch the rhythm). The rhyme translates into
English as "one two three, your dad is bald."

Here are two hay(na)ku by Oliver de la Paz:

Keats
writes darkly.
Birds trill unseen.

*

Watches
around wrists
make teeth marks.

In these and other works, what's evident is that the charge associated with
the haiku also can be present in the Pinoy form with the type of paradox
that one might find in the Filipino *bagoong*—a pungent fish sauce enjoyed
by Filipinos but, ahem, misunderstood by non-Filipinos. Thus, did
Filipino-American poet Catalina Cariaga also offer:

onion
just eaten;
smell my breath

*****

Most of the "Pinoy Haiku" came from writers who belonged to Flips, a listserve of Filipino writers or anyone interested in Filipino Literature that was co-founded by poets Nick Carbo and Vince Gotera. While they happily sent me what Vince called "Stairstep Tercets," my project also created a discussion on the implications of Naming—and how I was approaching it by using the phrase "Pinoy Haiku." Vince asked:

> *Appropriating the "haiku" name has all sorts of prosodic and postcolonial problems (by which I mean the WWII "colonizing" of the Philippines by Japan, among other things). Am I being overly serious here? When you say Kerouac refers to "American haiku" not having more than three words per line, I think he might have been reacting to Allen Ginsberg's "American sentence" which has 17 syllables per line. I guess my concern about calling it a "Pinoy haiku" is that readers could say, "Hey, Pinoys can't even get the haiku right!" They won't always have the Kerouac quote to guide them. Besides, why must we always be doing things in reaction to the term "American"? An interesting parallel poetic-form-naming might be Baraka's "low coup" form (the diametrical opposite of "high coup" / haiku). Maybe the Pinoy version could be the "hay (na)ku"?*

"Hay naku" is a common Filipino expression covering a variety of contexts—like the English word "Oh."

Another poet suggested that I also rename the project because the traditional haiku form should be respected. Well, yes and no. As I told that poet—I think that, in Poetry, rules are sometimes made to be broken.

Also, I initially wasn't moved by Vince's notion as regards Japan "colonizing" the Philippines during WWII. If anything, I thought that were I to consider that line of thinking (which I hadn't been), I didn't mind subverting the Japanese haiku form specifically because I thought of it as *talking back* against Japanese imperialism. But, on closer consideration, I realized that the perspective could work both ways... and that using the "haiku" reference also could imply a continuation of "colonial mentality."

Ultimately, I bowed to Vince's wisdom—after all, he is so much older than me *(Hello, Elder!)*—and renamed the form "hay(na)ku."

*****

Since the birth of hay(na)ku, there has been a hay(na)ku contest judged by Barbara Jane Reyes which was quite popular in the internet's poetry blogland; the hay(na)ku form was taught by Junichi P. Semitsu, then Director of "June Jordan's Poetry for the People" program at the African American Studies Department at U.C. Berkeley; the hay(na)ku has spread to the visual poetry and visual art worlds; and many poets and visual artists around the world—non-Filipino as well as Filipino—have picked up the form to write it as I originally conceived as well as to offer variations. As of 2018, the hay(na)ku has appeared in numerous literary journals and about 80 single-author poetry collections including 12 dedicated only to the hay(na)ku form as well as an all-Finnish hay(na)ku book. In 2017, I released from a Romanian publisher the trilingual limited edition *YOUR FATHER IS BALD* which presents some of my hay(na)ku in English with Romanian and Spanish translations. The form also has generated five different anthologies edited by six different editors. (More information is available at https://eileenrtabios.com/haynaku/)

The hay(na)ku also celebrated its 15th birthday in 2018, an event celebrated with readings, performances, exhibitions and a birthday cake at the San Francisco and Saint Helena Public Libraries. Birthday sponsors were Meritage Press, xPress(ed), Paloma Press, the two libraries and specifically San Francisco Public Library's Filipino American Center, and Philippine American Writers & Artists. For this year-long celebration, I am grateful to the hard work of Abraham Ignacio, Jr., Aileen Ibardaloza Cassinetto, Edwin Lozada, Melinda Luisa de Jesus, Michelle Bautista, and Abigail Licad, among others.

As the hay(na)ku's inventor, I welcome variations to the form which I propose to be flexible and welcoming. Among its variations (several of which are included in this collection) are:

—"reverse hay(na)ku" where the word count for the tercet is 3, 2, 1 instead of 1, 2, 3

—"chained hay(na)ku sequence" where the poem is comprised of more than one tercet

—"haybun" where the poem contains both tercet and prose

—"ducktail hay(na)ku" where a tercet or sequence of tercets is/are ended with a last stanza being a single line that can be as long as desired by the poet (the inspiration is a haircut where hair is trimmed short except for a long strand dangling from the middle of the back of the head)

—"Hay(na)ku Sonnet" by Vince Gotera, a form created through four hay(na)ku tercets plus an ending couplet with three words per line. The closing couplet is actually a hay(na)ku where the one-word line and the two-word line have been concatenated in order to end up with 14 lines

—"Rippled Mirror" hay(na)ku where the first tercet with a 1, 2, 3 word count is followed by a tercet with a 3, 2, 1 word count and where the narrative content is somewhat reversed between the two tercets

—"melting hay(na)ku" where the poem begins with the traditional tercet form before the stanzas "melt" into prose poetry paragraphs, sentences or fragments

—"The Mayan Hay(na)ku" created by then 11-year-old Maya Fink whereby the first line has a word comprised of one letter, the second line two words each comprised of two letters, the third line three words each comprised of three letters, and so on for as long as the poet cares to take it

—the internet's "moving hay(na)ku" proposed by Kari Kokko whereby, through the wonders of HTML, the lines move across the screen

—"abecedarian hay(na)ku" proposed by Scott Glassman where each word begins with each succeeding letter in the English alphabet

—"worm hay(na)ku" proposed by Ivy Alvarez who describes it as "using letters that don't have tops" (b, d, f, h, i, j, k, l, t) or tails (g, j, p, q, y)

—Tagalog slang hay(na)ku offered by Marlon Unas Esguerra

—"hay(na)ku with shadorma ending" created by Bastet of the blog *MindLoveMisery's Menagerie* (a shadorma is a Spanish poetic form)

—"hay(na)ku sentence" proposed by Jean Vengua who notes, "A sentence based on hay(na)ku is brief; it would slip by with perhaps less of a sense of 'finish,' yet it has a certain impact... Here's one: *Primaries are over; the crows alight.*"

—collaborations between poets and visual artists (which generated an anthology dedicated to such collaborations of three or more poets/ artists, *THE CHAINED HAY(NA)KU* (2012))

—and visual or sculptural forms of the hay(na)ku, from visual poetry to collages to paintings (e.g. Thomas Fink) to even a kitchen towel installation by Sandy and Barbara McIntosh.

*****

As one can see by the history of the hay(na)ku, it has succeeded in becoming a community-based poetic form; this fits my own thoughts on the poem as a space for engagement. Some favorite poetic projects are those where I helped create a community—through not just poetic content but also poetic form. I feel this way because I think a poem doesn't fully mature without a particular community called reader(s). Poetry is (inherently) social.

After the initial response by Filipino poets to the hay(na)ku, many—if not most—hay(na)ku have been written by non-Filipinos. This is certainly a fine result since Poetry is not (or need not be) ethnic-specific. But I'm also glad that non-Filipinos have taken up this form because I consider the hay(na)ku to be both a Filipino as well as Diasporic Poetic. I agree with Filipino poet and novelist Eric Gamalinda when he observes, "The history of the Philippines is the history of the world."

—Eileen R. Tabios

From *I Take Thee, English,*
For My Beloved, 2005

Weather Du Jour

blueness
of sky—
I am breathing

After Chazal

Sunflowers
release gold—
dust of illusion

Revvvv

poems
in belly—
fuel for flight

Athena

What's deemed necessary
changes. Hear
me

listening in another
decade, editing
last

and first lines.
A different
Singer

croons from behind
an impassive
speaker.

I listen, cross
out more
lines.

The poem cannot
be pure.
Sound

never travels unimpeded
by anonymous
butterflies.

Writing it down
merely freezes
flight—

Translation: an inevitable
fall. Take
control

by shooting it
as if
pigeons

were clay: This
one is.
But

it provided pleasure
once, was
"necessary."

Once, it flew
with non-imaginary
wings.

O, clay pigeon.
Translation: the
error

is my ear's.
The sky
ruptured

suddenly—I saw
but did
not

hear the precursor
fall of
leaves.

***

Edit it down.
Edit it
down.

Silence is Queen,
not lady
-in-waiting.

Edit it down.
Edit it.
Edit

it down. Edit
it. Edit.
Edit.

The Bread of Florence

We caught exciting
smells for
an

instant as we
passed—fresh
bread

from a *panetteria,*
the vinegary
tang

of a wineshop,
roasting coffee
from

a grocer's, new
leather from
a

saddler's—as well,
the frequent
whiff

of drains. When
a baker's boy
rings

a doorbell at
that tall
building,

shutters would be
flung open
from

above, and ebony-
long-haired, violet-eyed,
vanilla-scented,

raspberry-lipped, deep-dimpled, low-bloused
Marta would
lean

over the windowsill
cooing, "*Chi
e?*"

Then to save
a long
climb,

a basket on
a chord
would

fall, the bread
placed in
it,

and be hauled
up, hand
over

hand. Bread and
always a
letter—

his always-hungry proxy.

From *The Light Sang As It Left Your Eyes:*
Our Autobiography, 2007

Maganda Begins

"Maganda" is not just a Tagalog word that means "beautiful". "Maganda" is also the name of the first woman in a Filipino creation myth.

My love. If
words can
reach

whatever world you
suffer in—
Listen:

I have things
to tell
you.

At this muffled
end to
another

year, I prowl
somber streets
holding

you—in my
head, this
violence!—

a violent gaze.
You. With
dusk

arrives rain drifting
aslant like
premature

memory. Am I
the one
who

suddenly cleared these
streets? *My*
Love,

all our hours
are curfew
hours—

what I offer
is this
dying

fish into whose
gullet I
have

thrust my thumb.
Why did
you

lose all Alleluias?
My love—
Listen:

From *The Singer and Others:*
Flamenco Hay(na)ku, 2007

Sangre Negra / Black Blood

How does a
small tree
kill

a big tree?
The way
Vincent

Romero died onstage
dancing one
more

escobilla. Ole! Ayan!
The way
cantaores

drown in their
own blood
singing

one last letra.
Ole! How
does

a small tree
kill a
big

tree? His smell
like the
first

time: sweat and
marijuana. Oranges.
Cloves.

How does a
small tree
kill

a big tree?
Fall of
blue

—black hair. How
does a
small

tree kill? He
was nicknamed
"Bullet"

for his bald
head and
thick

neck, all smooth
except where
puckered

a long scar
documenting the
flight

of a gunshot.
How does
a…?

So moved he
ripped off
his

shirt. So moved
she clawed
her

cheeks. How does
a small
tree

kill a tree
so big
its

roots encircle the
entire planet?
How…

wither all red
roses into
insects?

How? You never
answer to
outsiders.

Drape black velvet
over the
Sun.

Dame La Verdad

Old and frail,
a sugar
sculpture

in a world
threatened by
storms.

But the real
shock was
her

feet, as misshapen
as I
imagine

the bound feet
of Chinese
women

might have been.
My future
beckoned—

the aborted wings
long have
wreaked

memory and desire
against my
back.

My poor back,
its skin
continuously

gathering to fatten
the puckering
nubs

atop each collarbone.
The claws
ending

her feet. The
fists bunched
on

my back from
reined-in wings.
We

are connoisseurs of
secrets, the
biggest

secret being how
we lost
all

rights to pray,
"Lord, have
mercy"

once we lost
desire for
mercy.

Bait The Dark Angel By

saying "Lizard" or
avoiding the
touch

of iron, or
choosing a
black

dog. Mama stood
as straight
as

only a true
Flamenca can.
She

pulled the dress
over her
head,

careful not to
stain it
with

her blood. In
the moonlight
I

saw how my
mother's bleak
eyes

had swollen and
turned purple.
But

she licked her
teeth and
smiled

when her tongue
discovered none
missing.

The floor was
checkered with
green

and lavender tiles.
He pointed
at

Mama's eyes and
joked, "Chop
up

those plums. The
sangria needs
more

fruit." Everyone laughed.
Mama laughed
loudest—

a laughter bearing
the harshness
of

aborted histories. Then
all crowded
around

Mama, repining her
still blue
-black

hair, snagging loops
of oiled
strands

from either side
of her
face

to camouflage her
bruised eyes,
giving

her glasses of
aguardiente to
kill

that which cannot
be killed.
Once,

he wondered if
she'd been
formed

from molten gold.
Touched, she
bore

what can never
be killed.
Outside—

perhaps beyond the
scarlet mountain—
perhaps

just beyond the
other side
of

that dirty window—
a bark
then

a prolonged howling
shriveling the
coward

's lungs. She
bore what
cannot

be killed: the
oversized heart
of

her dance: Pain.
Poetry. Blood.
You.

You. Blood. Poetry.
Pain. Her
Dance.

The Singer

When they heard
him, they
heard

the whips over
his ancestors
as

they were forced
out from
India.

They heard a
man thrown
into

jail for stealing
a small
bunch

of grapes, then
the ugly
grunts

of his starving
wife and
children.

When they heard
him, "they
heard

a shivering woman
with no
defense

as the soldiers
came to
do

what they did
with her
and

her still too-young
daughters." They
heard

the stars fall
into bleak
silence.

When they heard
him, they
heard

his cante come
from him
like

a rusty nail
being pulled
from

an old board.
La voz
afilla—

sandpaper voice. Good
Gitano voice:
Muy

rajo, very rough.
Do you
know

the worst thing
one can
say

about someone in
flamenco? No
me

dice nada. He
didn't say
anything

to me. He
didn't speak
something

I realized I
feared but
needed

to hear. Ay!
All these
stanzas

are rough! Or
worse, too
gentle.

They fumble. Earnest
as cows
and

they fumble. Do
you know
what

would be the
worst thing
said

about my poetry?
I created
nothing

that moved you.
Made you
cry

as if pain
was the
only

proof possible for
being alive.
So

who among you
listening will
be

the wild dog
I am
calling?

Show me your
snarl. Reveal
your

fangs. How can
I sing
blood

if I don't
bleed? Show
me

yourself as the
one for
whom

I will rip
my own
skin.

Show yourself before
you bore
me

with your patient
stalking. Show
yourself

darkened further by
my orders.
My

people trained me.
There is
no

shame in begging
for what
will

part my lips—
what will
trade

caresses with my
tongue—what
will

battle my teeth
and make
me

sweat. My people
trained me.
I

learned knives are
sharp by
being

cut. I learned
fires are
hot

by being burned.
I learned
to

stamp my heels
to sound
like

a machine-gun blast
because…*because*…
Show

yourself—I have
a song
to

turn you into
ice, then
shatter!

Ole! Verdad! Show
yourself—do
you

think I'm begging
for a
crust

of bread already
half-eaten by
cockroaches?!

As If

There was un
momento, a
poem

I wrote while
driving the
car.

My ego would
not let
me

pull over to
jot it
down.

"If a poem
is so
powerful

it will return,"
I have
boasted

for a long
time to
other

poets, as if
I possessed
some

knowledge they did
not already
know.

It feels like
years and
yet

that poem has
not yet
returned.

What I recall
is that,
somehow,

it related to
perfect timing
y

flamenco.

La Loca

*In the green
morning I
wanted*

*to be a
heart. A
heart.*

*And at evening's
end, I
wanted*

*to be my
voice. A
nightingale.
—LO(R)CA*

She fell in
love. Poor
Juana.

Fell in love
with the
most

handsome man in
the kingdom.
How

did the Prince
requite her
love?

By betraying her
with every
woman

who simpered across
his path.
By

lashing a florid
sky across
her

skin. By cutting
her beautiful
hair.

Poor Juana—always
looking behind
her

stooped shoulders. How
her Prince
mocked

her, chilling her
tears into
multiple

strands of pearls.
Still, when
he

died, Juana went
mad. She
clawed

her cheeks and
confused dogs
into

whimpers, then howls.
She rode
throughout

Granada keening over
her Prince's
coffin

in a gloomy
carriage pulled
by

eight horses. She
rode and
rode

with his stench
becoming hers
until

they both stunk
up all
of

Espana. She refused
to bury
him,

begging faces she
concocted from
receding

knotholes of trees
passed by
their

carriage, begging faces
she drew
by

connecting the stars
pockmarking the
irritated

night sky, begging
faces she
surfaced

from bonfire smokes
and crumpled
balls

of sodden handkerchiefs.
Her plea?
She

pleaded for his
resurrection.
Bah.

She pleaded as
if he
would

return to her
if he
came

to breathe again.
Bah. As
if

he once was
there for
her.

As if he
ever wrote
Poetry

for her. Now,
do not
misunderstand:

We gitanas adore
Juana The
"Crazy".

To honor her,
we cross
ourselves

and touch our
hair. We
honor

her because Juana
never faltered
from

living her Truth
even as
lies

snuffed the votive
lights in
her

eyes. Dame la
verdad. Poor
Juana.

> *Once, I stepped*
> *into a*
> *story…*

I love Juana.
But I
loathe

her, too. Once,
I courted
madness

for Poetry. But
I punched
through

that blur—grew
back my
hair.

Does it matter
that its
harvest

now elicits snow?
I punched
through

that silver, shimmery
blur. Ole!
I

grew back my
hair! So
what

if Winter has
become my
veil?

>   *I thought the*
>   *story was*
>   *mine…*

I grew back
my hair.
I

love my refuge.
It veils
me

into believing that
when I
write

of Juana The
Mad, I
am

still young with
glossy, blue-black
hair.

That when I
write my
poems

Juana is a
subject and
not

the one releasing
the wind
that

flares my skirts
high to
reveal

absolutely furious footwork
—en compas—
conjuring

up the ghosts
of those
who

laugh at my
red eyes—
dark

angels who taught:
there is
no

madness. There is
only a
woman

brutishly in love.
Hear me
read

me singing to
You the
A.

The E. The
I. The
O.

The U. The
You. The
U.

And the Y.
Hear me
and

Juana dance! The
seduction of
flowers

blossoming into vowels.
Hear me
y

Juana sing the
machinegun blast
of

The A, The
I, The
E,

The O, The
U. Hear
us

die from the
Song of
Y,

the Dance of
Why? Listen
all

you nightingales! Why?
I curse
all

you nightingales! Why?
En compas/s!
I

thought it was
only a
story.

I thought the
story was
mine:

a bird caws
from my
mirror.

My mirror spits
out bloodied
feathers.

I love you
nightingales! All
of

you! Why, dear
nightingales? Why?
Y

WHY? Y WHY?

From *Footnotes to Algebra: Uncollected Poems 1995-2009*, 2009

The Hay(na)ku of Numbers

One
need not
rely on anyone

unless
One wants
to relax melancholy

though
such dilution
is mere rest

never
the multiplication
of One beyond

One

*****

Two
is not
one or three

but
two can
be a sum

***

Three
is you
cheating on me

or
making love
with much generosity

***

Four
is tricky:
It can split

into
two camps:
"X" versus "Z"

***

Five
may not
be your favorite

as
five enables
one left out

***

Six
is simple:
it simply is.

***

Seven
will never
betray. Trust me.

***

Eight
is hourglass
frittering sand away

but
done so
elegantly as to

generate
no complaints
again and again

and
again and
again and again

***

Nine
is odd
without one more

*****

Ten
is one
opened up to

potential.

On A Pyre: An Ars Poetica

Flames
eating my
body hotter than

fire
for the
poetry in burning

books
ravage more
than a drought-stricken

forest's
revenge for
the creation of

paper
so flimsy
against non-metaphorical needs—

From *The Chained Hay(na)ku Project*, 2012

Four Skin Confessions

Collaboration by Ivy Alvarez, John Bloomberg-Rissman, Ernesto Priego and Eileen R. Tabios

1a)

The
body judges
better than the

mind.
In the
Great Silent Calm

that
always follows,
the afternoon went

soft
and gold,
gold and soft,

on
the slopes
of the dry

San
Gabriels, where
spindle-hag scrub

scratch
out an
odd cuneiform on

the
sky — i.e.
En arche en

ho
logos, kai
ho logos en

pros
ton theon,
kai theos en

ho
logos. Sous
rature. We get

to
carry each
other, carry each

other.
Hey hey …
sha la la.

Sun-
stung shores
ribbon radio snatches.

Trees
catch sound
to throw it

back.
The body
turns, changes colo(u)r.

I've
fallen I've
fallen into the

book
I've fallen
into the book

of
my body.
… I can't get

up.
Mind judges
the weary body

reading
the lines
on palms and

fingers
and trees
sway like children

bored
in libraries
abandoned by parents

tired
as usual
of the wind.

Each
book stays
still like clay,

while
the moon
pretends to marry

signing
her name
with purple blood.

Think
of it
this way: bodies

dream
with hojas,
libros y árboles.

I've
fallen
into the tropical

moondance
of palm
trees: "had I

not
kept fire
for myself, I'd

have
nothing to
call my own".

And
also for
stretching the spine.

I
read books
looking for You.

I
write books
to quell pronouns

separating
our bodies
from trees, wind,

sky
into mere
letters, all misspelled.

All
of you
alchemizing libraries from

veins
riotous, plentiful
but filling only

one
leaf, sundering
green for gold —

where
ground crumbles,
a specific intimacy.

1b)

*Olam
u-melo'o, a
world and the*

*fullness
thereof, that
you would kiss*

*me
with the
kisses of your*

mouth,
that we
would burn away

all
pronouns, that
we would ride

that
cherub of
light and float

in
18,000 worlds,
listening to heavenly

DJs,
that we
would strut the

widest
Broadways of
our biggest cities,

heads
wrapped in
copper snakes, because

"Copper
snakes are
the right idea …

they
have a
potential for healing."

Books
and bodies.
Words and worlds.

They
suck you
in, digest you

like
heads swallowed
by shy anacondas.

"I
know this
much is true."

Still —
let's not
circle the bush:

reuniting
us here,
in this place,

here
and in
what little time

we
share here,
this deliberate gathering,

is
simply
friendship,

like
the roots
of the forests

of
Manila or
swamps in Florida

or
the dark
rivers of Oaxaca.

Go
there where
you cannot, I

beg
you, as
your friend, like

that
brujo over
there in Catemaco,

who
once predicted
bodies and books

and
trees full
of foreign blood:

hear
where nothing
rings or sounds,

mad
poets, because
"the most impossible

is
possible", in
litteris, this confession.

2)

Hear
where nothing
is said. Here

where
everything worth
hearing is offered.

En
arche en
ho logos, kai

ho …
the bush
suddenly ablaze, sky

flaming
in your
eyes and mine,

blood
melting to
ink in our

veins,
then leaking
to shape gold

letters
on correspondence
masquerading as books.

Here
where Nothing
is said, hear

where
Nothing is
said, watch smoke rise

off
the tongue,
words like snakes.

The
tongue is
a golden page.

No
golden age,
no smoky page,

no
gold-tongued
rage against dying,

blood
flaming, ink
dyeing, drying, dying.

(Time
stops. Glittering
blackness. First day

after
a coma.
A place like

Wales.
Music, images
of loveable skin.

I've
fallen out
of the body.)

In
the beginning
was the body,

bebed,
porque este
es mi cuerpo,

flesh
made word,
red like wine.

But
can faux
bushes exist in

poems
if gold
includes circumcision and

its
multicultural confessions?
Circumfession (once again?)

experienced
physically as
circumcision without a

single flinch from
allowing the
descent

of the blade.
Nor does
a single

nerve end
flinch.
Indeed,

a grin surfaces,
so perverse
is

hir
funny bone.
Believe it, Honey,

as
a Mohel,
I would bare

proudly-filed,
pyramid-shaped teeth
you didn't know

hid
behind lips
crimson with lipstick

and
wine and
blood and ink

and
Derrida and
confessions and those

which
never will
be confessed and…

3)

Flick
the dial.
Spicer Satellite Radio:

" …we
must not
let the paths

of
desire become
overgrown … I am

only
counting on
what comes of

my
own openness,
my eagerness to

wander
in search
of everything … it

keeps
me in
mysterious communication with

other
open beings,
as if we

were
suddenly called
to assemble…" [slow fade…]

"That
was André
the Pope singing

that
old surrealist
classic, Mad Love.

And
now…" Change
the station? Nah.

My
lost highway
bends into a

sunset
sky dripping
a thousand mingled

shades
of lipstick,
blood and wine.

Such
dry air —
all the beers

of
San Miguel
will not slake,

dark and bitter,
my thirst
blank,

unspooling as roads
go, no
signals,

flesh nothing but
a limbic
afterthought.

What colo(u)r is
your flesh?
Unpick

these new stitches,
like stark
dashes,

down a lipsticked,
wined, blooded
road.

Jerry,
in London,
he told John:

"We blew Monterey
and Woodstock:
bang

crash roar,
then Hendrix set

fire to everything,
then we
whooooosh…"

This
note will
sustain as long

as you like.
The next
Step

is
the note
that catches, the

last form is,
by far,
hardest

to
achieve. Once
you play this

loud,
the entire
stage becomes sensitive

to feedback: celestial
tone, crimson
kiss.

Song
of crimson
kisses kissing crimson

into you until
your flesh
crimsons

from osmosis with
bloodied bloody
words.

The colo(u)r of
my flesh?
Word.

4)

This
moves like
a festival now.

The mud the
crowd the
mosh

the
fire. My
flesh? My flesh,

that word that's
so … that's
so …

I
lost my
body once, on

2000 mics and
an endless
celestial

crimson
feedback burning
bush Garcia solo,

and I laughed,
because … I
DIDN'T

NEED
IT. But
I needed it

later. I need
it now.
What

colo(u)r
is my
flesh? Word. What

word? I don't
know. All
I

know:
only you
can speak it.

Speak my flesh
into your
microphone,

flesh
is word
is love, Love.

Here's the sound
of my
skin

blooming
crimson kisses,
kissing shady desire,

stars underfoot, words
hang above,
constellar

sunshine,
la crème
de la créme,

the milky way
of skin
written

with
birth spots
a divine battle

and all I
do is
worship

scars,
ever-more scars —
how do you

measure the years?
Never healed
scars —

impossible scars, impossible
scars bloomed
to

fruit
by poetry
which doesn't heal

but compels you
to keep
breathing.

Breathe
through anything
and everything thrown

at you by
even the
stars —

suddenly miserable points
of light
which

can't help but
illumine. Scars
seared

with the most
crimson-ridden
light.

Like
refusing to
put I love

you under erasure.
Keep on
dancing

until
daylight ... as
Sherril Jaffe wrote

those
many years
ago, "Scars make

your
body more
interesting." Impossible scars

bloomed to fruit,
sticky-sweet,
seed-

bearing ...
Rest, and
look at this

goddamned red wheelbarrow.
Whatever it
is.

5)

Forgive
me, you
were delicious cold

or ... well, so
much depends
on ...

forgive
me, you
were so warm,

so
good to
dance near your

raised
flesh, the tracks
sewn over, scars

tell
stories, all
they know, time

punctuates
the skin.
Here you are.

Here
I am
with a story

of abiding love,
because there
are

flowers
also in
hell, and I

cannot cross out
your name,
scarred,

inked
over this
skin you once

made only yours
by kissing,
"I

didn't know
tattoos were felt,"

you told me
that night
we

read
The Torah
looking for the

beginning of your name,
Raquel, who
Waited

for
years for
love, abiding love,

and the candles
died out,
slowly

dripping
white blood
over your earrings,

until one day
you did
not

forget
them here,
but your fingers

traced the name,
the tracks
of

my
story, literally
raised flesh, Darling.

What do I
remember, remember,
that

was
shaped as
this thing we

are still afraid
to call
love?

6)

What I forgot
and now
remember

because you love
me (and
me)

is why I answered
Homer's Odyssey
and Iliad

when an anthology
editor asked
for

favorite books which
influenced my
poetry.

I recalled Homer's
books not
just

for their words
but their
"physicality."

In my birthland
_____ _____
books

were/are expensive.
A bookshelf
Held

Glory in our
living room.
Mama

ensured we children
understood that
treasures

lived on those
shelves: Odyssey,
Iliad,

many more books.
Even now
My

fingers itch remembering
the edges
of pages

as I leafed
through their
stories,

words blooming flesh
touching other
flesh.

But let me
recall, too,
a twin:

the horror ever
lurking within
my

mind, my body:
me and
You!

:Something else was
born that
day

when I first
tip-toed to
reach

for my first
book to
read.

When I began
to write
Poetry

I had nothing
to say.
And

I thought that
okay. Many
Masters

in the poetry
universe had
proclaimed:

Poetry is not
meaning, but
language.

Relatedly, the authors
died. So
I

concocted fiction for
my poems,
often

dark tales since
one must
be

dramatic, no? But
then I
began

to live those
stories with
nothing

less than my
own body.
                    stars—

          suddenly miserable points
          of light
          which

           can't help but
          illumine. Scars
          seared

          with the most
          crimson-ridden
          light.

Snow

spread through my
veins until
my

eyes blossomed crimson.
No Master
Ever

warned me: in
Poetry, someone
Always

speaks. Someone always
feels. Someone
always

bleeds. Someone always
scars. Someone
often

with bared teeth.
No one
warned:

in Poetry, Dear
One(s), this
Poet

may concoct fiction,
but will
never

lie. Come, Darling,
see my
beautiful

eyes. See how
anguish has
bled

my eyes bright.
See how
Anguish

surfaced snow in
my crimson
vision.

See how poetry
lit me
purple

from within, then
turned me
blind.

Preface

While no one really knows the number of orphans worldwide, a common estimate is 147 million. These children represent one of the biggest humanitarian tragedies of our time even as their plight fails to receive as much attention as natural disasters or wars.

147 Million Orphans: MMXI-MML is the first book-length haybun poetry collection. A "haybun" is a combination of hay(na)ku and other text.

For these haybun, the opening hay(na)ku tercet generally served as impetus to the subsequent prose. Each word forming the hay(na)ku tercets is taken from a school project by Eileen R. Tabios' adopted son, Michael (with Michael's permission). After arriving in the United States, Michael had been encouraged to learn English in 8th grade partly by learning 25 new words a week.

Haybun MMXIII

television
screening insightful
prescient melancholy evasive

If you were a sleeping bird in Madagascar, a certain species of moth might drink your tears through a fearsome proboscis shaped like a harpoon. They'd insert their tools beneath your eyelids. They would drink avidly. You were a rapt presence as you met this species through the grainy television screen used to babysit hundreds of orphans. After the television darkened, no genius would be required to explain your prescient conclusion: you will attempt to evade too much in this life, you will fail, there is no other life. ~~You, sadly, will come to prefer silk, even polyester, doppelgangers to roses that otherwise would shrivel.~~ Your insights will always arise from the sheen of rain-drenched pavements. For example, that one can weep without the aid of nightmares—that one can weep in the most safe haven, or even the small heavens that still and do manage to pock-mark our mortal planet.

Haybun MMXIV

regurgitate
bake jargon
laconic nefarious dainty

She remained grateful, even when the celebrity couple edited the only gift she could give her child: a name. The darkness revealed a stench of copper and dirt—it worsened to form a man. The darkness revealed a dagger. The darkness revealed a hand duct-taping her lips as her body was invaded as if it contained missiles. The darkness lifted to reveal Awasa, a town in southern Ethiopia, seemingly as it was before a night began and ended into someone else's story. She named the consequence, "Yemsrach"—she named the consequence as if the infant was always intended. She named the baby "Good News." She became the gift renamed "Zahara." Her name is Mentwabe Dawit—she will kiss tabloid pictures of Angelina Jolie. Her child who bears the names of two different stories is no longer malnourished. Her child has ceased dying. Her child is now proactively living, with laughter no stranger. Her name is Mentwabe Dawit—the daughter of another woman who defied their culture where rape is taboo for all participants. Certain details must be named to be plucked out of the silence camouflaged as background to someone else's story. What is the name of the mother who continued to love her daughter after a rape? The mother who counseled her daughter to continue living despite the world they inherited versus chose—what is her name? (Someday, Zahara will want to know.) ~~The mother who would not let Mentwabe Dawit's body become a civil war~~—what is her name! (Someday, Zahara will want to know.) The mother who would not let Mentwabe Dawit's body become a civil war—what is her name!

Haybun MMXV

quibble
malignant integrate
limp conceptualize prioritize

To remember a father's fist against a mother's cheek is to integrate
the malignant into myocardium. Short-term memory is a temporary
activation of neural connections that can store incidents for mere seconds.
Short-term memories become long-term through continued recall and
associations that change the nerves' physical structure. The adoption
therapist is eager for hir continued attention. But isn't the adoptee simply
protecting his body? Long-term memory bases its existence on biology.
The adoption therapist brushes away my parental concern as a quibble.
Adoption is an industry, as commercial as the polyethylene commodities
traveling on ship tankers from China with no regard for carbon footprints.
Yes, one can leave footprints on water. Recall Jesus. And how his father
counseled adoption as the camel's key for passing through the needle's
eye. I became a mother through ~~someone else's~~ more than one person's
loss. I see the rose and feel the thorn. I cannot protect my sons and
daughters. But they will be sons and daughters: I give them the Word, and
the word is the non-harrowing—and even delicious!— "Mom"! I feel the
thorn and see the rose: the crown that, when worn, begins a bleeding so
lyrical it most assuredly will move the most addicted bees to leave their
sodden Queen.

Haybun MMXX

scenario
unsaturated orchardist
unclothed anechdotist anachronistic

…remains an orphan. Due to silence. She cannot utter the word "Mom." Somewhere, a lily unfurled to reveal a red pistil so passionate a camera can reconfigure it into a lipstick named Alejandra. Since the petal forever hides it from possible views, it might as well be named Wound. Alejandra remembers her childhood and says adamantly with a moue of her adultly plump lips, "I don't miss it." Yet she cannot articulate a doorway into a future ~~she believes is healthy but which~~ she cannot desire. I understand: the adoptive parent can never be joyful over lessons attained through a child's loss. Damn those lilies and their hidden penises. Damn those lies and the sunlit parallel universes so baldly cancelled. Damn those sterile orchards. Damn those anecdotes that can never satisfy. Damn how silences become solids. Insert the phrase: *STILL TO BE EDITED.* Entonces, damn those second-guessings to no avail, where every gesture is a moment of nakedness. Thus, fragile

Haybun MMXXII

cleroy
plague itinerant
coenzyme vagabond harass

Your desire to please me led you to learn my tongue. You did not know to judge the promiscuity of my language—it even insists on poetry after the ~~concentration camps~~ expulsion of 147 million orphans. That there is no Paradise is irrelevant. You focused on the hollow of my neck— the permanence of its perfumed *Welcome!* whenever a shadow harasses your eyes and you need nothing less than maternal embrace. Tell me as many words as you learn ~~even~~ especially the vagabonds: *cleroy, schmeroy…* the words themselves do not matter. Poetry is not words, and I gladly coenzyme you in Chanel No. 5 song as we celebrate what your future will not become (even as it foretells that 147 million is merely a square root): *itinerant.*

From *To Be An Empire Is To Burn*, 2017

FERDINAND EDRALIN MARCOS
(Rippled Mirror Hay(na)ku #1)

"Power
corrupts absolutely"—
you provided proof.

Your life proved
"Absolute corruption
powers."

On Green Lawn, the Scent of White

No promises exist
in combat…
Hot

lead muzzle velocity
= 1,000 feet/second…
Proverbial

bad shit? Bound
to happen…
Rare

constant: white marble
tombstones… From
afar

eyes imagine magnolias
against grass…
But

he faces warrior's
mother over
closed

casket… "I made
him promise
to

stay alive"… Medals
fail to
console…

"War makes promises
difficult." He
offers

flag folded, not
waving…
 "General,

are you good?
You survived…"
Truth

is impossible: *Only*
the dead
soldier

is good. He
catches scent
of

the past with
its white
blossoms…

Once, he was
a boy,
playing

in his mother's
garden… Generals
age

from their knowledge.
Silently, he
begs

the grieving mother…
Don't let
me

explain: flowers
must be
crushed

for perfume…

From *Menopausal Hay(na)ku for P-Grubbers*, 2017

Hay Naku! That Menopause!
—after No. 45

(#1)
Men—
O pause:
Reconsider, then begin

(#2)
Men—
O pause:
Apparently, its "deepest

Truths
are hot
flashes, barely suppressed

rage
and memory
loss." "Drump who?"

(#3)
Men—
O pause:
On the other

hand
I feel
quite proud of

my
hot flashes.
I feel amazed

over
generating so
much heat. I

think,
drenched in
sweat, I could

absolutely
warm up
an entire city!

(#4)
Men—
O pause:
When memory loss

begins
happening regularly,
you stop wanting

conversation—
You may
forget your point

before
you finish
your sentence! [PAUSE]

"What
happens when
dementia becomes politicized?"

But
He cannot
excuse himself by

using
women for
their words, like

"Sorry,
it's my
menopause brain." SAD!

(#5)
Men—
O pause:
Female CEOs demanding

through
my phone:
"I am losing

my
mind. I
need help **NOW!**"

(#6):
Men—
O pause:
When Angelina Jolie

courageously
decided to
remove ovaries and

breasts
because she
risked breast and

ovarian
cancer, reaction
included concern she

might
enter menopause
early. But she

objected,
pushing back
against the narrative

menopause
is unwelcome,
pushing back definitively

against
the narrative
aging is bad.

Angie,
Thank you!
You remain beautiful.

(#7)
Men—
O pause:
How wonderful if

we
all got
to a place

where
we can
share in these

conversations
openly and
without shame. So

others
can understand
we are not

Insane!

(#8)
Men—
O pause:
My "menopause brain"—

when
I own
it out loud

fear
lessens. Don't
we often fear

what
we don't
acknowledge, or know?

(#9)
Men—
O pause:
I repeat, I

can
warm up
an entire city!

(#10)
Men—
O pause:
I regret nothing.

From *Your Father Is Bald: Selected Hay(na)ku Poems*, 2017

The Ineffability of Mushrooms

(A Novella-in-Verse)

1)
The porcini appeared
under right
conditions:

after heavy rain
soaked warm
earth—

this desired combination
lovingly labeled
"smoke."

2)
F____ gave us
a wicker
basket

of loose weave
so that
after

mushrooms were collected
spoor could
escape

to fertilize earth
as we
continued

to harvest. "Give
always to
those

who offer gifts
first and
generously."

3)
We never found
huge quantities
like

those claimed by
many mushroom
hunters.

But he reminded:
Italians invent
mushroom

stories like British
fishermen do
fishing.

4)
For hunting truffles,
Italians prefer
dogs

over pigs who
are so
greedy

they are almost
impossible to
control

once they've scented
a truffle.
Taking

his dog to
a likely
spot

the hunter spurs
him on
with

cries—*Dai! Dai!*
Cerca!—like
those

of a *cacciatore*
after gamebirds.
White

truffles can grow
down 15
inches.

When the dog
begins scratching,
his

handler immediately pulls
him away
otherwise

his eager paws
will wreak
havoc

upon the mushrooms.
The Sublime
rarely

allows shortcuts.
The handler
himself

must get down
on all
fours

to sniff for
scents of
must—

he is irreplaceable
when digging
carefully—

so very care-full-y…

5)
We watched F____
slice mushrooms
delicately

then spread thin
segments on
wood

planks to dry
under the
sun.

Afterwards, they were
stored in
muslin

or calico bags
near the
kitchen

fireplace. Later in
London, I
received

each Autumn one
precious, single
bag

of dried mushrooms
and memories
then

lingering like smoke.
The last
arrived

in 1939, shortly
after the
outbreak

of war.

From *One, Two, Three: Selected Hay(na)ku Poems / Uno, dos, tres: Selección de Hay(na)kus*, 2018

DIE WE DO

Die
we do
as much as

we
live. Then
we write: right

what
we lived
when we write.

Morir hacemos

Morir:
lo hacemos
tanto como vivir.

Entonces,
nosotros escribimos:
corregimos aquello que

vivimos
cuando, así,
nosotros lo escribimos.

(Spanish translation by Rebeka Lembo)

III. MURDER DEATH RESURRECTION

I choose to remember...

—Eileen R. Tabios

Generating the MDR Tercets

In the immediate aftermath of inventing the hay(na)ku, I could not approach the tercet form in a conventional way, that is, by writing directly in it. My project "Murder Death Resurrection" (MDR), which created my "MDR Poetry Generator," offered me a path of taking it slant: lines from the MDR Poetry Generator provided a scaffolding for new tercets. The following essay introduces the MDR Poetry Generator which describes its poems as containing lines that all begin with "I Forgot"—an example is the poem from 44 RESURRECTIONS. On the other hand, the tercets from HIRAETH: Tercets From the Last Archipelago coalesced by riffing off lines from the MDR Poetry Generator while foregoing "I forgot..." for the unstated "I choose to remember...".

***

A five-year (2013-2018) project, "Murder Death Resurrection" (MDR), includes "The MDR Poetry Generator" that brings together much of my poetics and poet tics. The MDR Poetry Generator contains a data base of 1,167 lines which can be combined randomly to make a large number of poems; the shortest would be a couplet and the longest would be a poem of 1,167 lines. Examples of couplets and longer forms are available in *44 RESURRECTIONS*, the first poetry collection emanating from the MDR Poetry Generator. *AMNESIA: Somebody's Memoir* is a single poem of 1,167 lines or verse-novel (I like disrupting, or intervening, in the fixity of forms as I believe Poetry is an unstable terrain).

The MDR Poetry Generator's conceit is that any combination of its 1,167 lines succeeds in creating a poem. Thus, I can create—generate—new poems unthinkingly from its database. For example, I created several of the poems in *44 RESURRECTIONS* by blindly pointing at lines on a print-out to combine. While the poems cohere partly by the scaffolding of beginning each line with the phrase "I forgot..." (a tactic inspired by reading Tom Beckett's fabulous poem "I Forgot" in his book ~~DIPSTICK~~ *(DIPTYCH)*, Marsh Hawk Press, 2014), these poems reflect long-held interests in abstract and cubist language (partly as a means to interrogate English whose narrative once was a colonizing tool over my birth land, the Philippines). Through my perceptions of abstraction and cubism, I've written poems whose lines are not fixed in order and, indeed, can be reordered (when I began writing poems, I was very interested in the prose poem form and in writing paragraphs that can be reordered within the poem).

Yet while the MDR Poetry Generator presents poems not generated through my personal preferences, the results are not distanced from the author: I created the 1,167 lines from reading through 27 previously-published poetry collections—the title's references to murder, death and resurrection reflect the idea of putting to death the prior work, only to resurrect them into something new: sometimes, creation first requires destruction. But if randomness is the operating system for new poems (i.e. the lines can be combined at random to make new poems), those new poems nonetheless contain all the personal involvement—and love!—that went into the writing of its lines. The results dislocate without eliminating authorship.

Curious about the number of poems (in math, permutations) possible from these 1,167 lines, I asked my son's high school math tutor, Carl Ericson, to calculate it for me. Carl used an approximation formula to estimate that the total poems possible to be generated by the MDR Poetry Generator is a number that has 3,011 digits. Subsequently, Carl's estimate would be affirmed by Errol Koenig, a student at Johns Hopkins Applied Mathematics & Statistics department. Errol derived the number through the equation 1146!-1146, a number that roughly rounds to 1.129300103 E+3010 [that is, 1.129300103 times 10 to the 3,010th power] – a 3,011-digit number! (The number of lines initially was believed to be 1,146, but the result would be similar for 1,167.) Since the number of permutated poems is huge, this means I can keep ~~writing~~ making poems for the rest of my life without having to write new text. Are the poems any good? Using publication as a means of answering that question, the poems are just like my other non-generated poems: despite some rejections, there are also acceptances such that a significant number has found publication homes.

As of this writing, The MDR Project has generated about 160 poems, including those that make up five books, four chapbooks and one mini-book. Some poems also generated visual poetry versions, such as "I Forgot Forgetting My Skin Was Ruin" which inaugurated *h&*, a journal of visual/concrete poetry, and "Excavating the Filipino In Me" which was exhibited in "CHROMATEXT REBOOTED," a visual poetry and arts show organized by the Philippine Literary Arts Council at the Cultural Center of the Philippines, Manila (Nov. 6, 2015-Jan. 17, 2016). The latter project also resulted in a chapbook, *EXCAVATING THE FILIPINO IN ME* (Tinfish Press, Hawai'i, 2016).

***

The MDR Poetry Generator also reflects what I call "Kapwa Poetics"—a poetics based on indigenous Filipino practices. There's an image from pre-colonial Philippine times of a human standing with a hand lifted upwards; if you happened to be at a certain distance from the man and took a snapshot, it would look like the human was touching the sky. In a poetics essay in my book *THE AWAKENING* (theenk books, New York, 2013), I'd described the significance of this image as:

"...the moment, the space, from which I attempt to create poems. In the indigenous myth, the human, by being rooted onto the planet but also touching the sky, is connected to everything in the universe and across all time, including that the human is rooted to the past and future—indeed, there is no unfolding of time. In that moment, all of existence—past, present and future—has coalesced into a singular moment, a single gem with an infinite expanse. In that moment, were I that human, I am connected to everything so that there is nothing or no one I do not know. I am everyone and everything, and everything and everyone is me. In that moment, to paraphrase something I once I heard from some Buddhist, German or French philosopher, or Star Trek character, 'No one or nothing is alien to me.'"

Within this indigenous moment or space, both intentionalized authorship and the randomness with which the lines are combined from The MDR Poetry Generator are irrelevant—*All is One and One is All.*

Thrice, I Forgot (1-20)

I forgot moths as the sun disappeared—"the flutter of wings as they teased a dim porch light."

I forgot entrancement with the layered auras of decay.

I forgot a water lily forms instantaneously.

***

I forgot releasing breath solely to describe milk transformed by your scent.

I forgot Tequila Corazon de Agave alchemized from the heart of blue agave bred in the rich, red soil of the "Highlands" in Arandas, Jalisco, Mexico.

I forgot "Mutual Funds" is an oxymoron.

***

I forgot the seduction of wet cobblestones.

I forgot the blinding whiteness of a thick porcelain mug sunning itself on your windowsill.

I forgot *those* dolls—for a moment, their eyes had relaxed.

***

I forgot how dusk enhanced conversations—

I forgot the seams caused by bindings—

I forgot the perfume of fresh bread as we passed a *panetteria*, the vinegary tang floating out of a wine shop, heaven as the scent of roasting coffee from a grocer, and the necessary reminder of those different from us through the stench of street drains—

***

I forgot the conundrums of evacuating mornings—

I forgot Clementina stuffing Rosa with candied chestnuts in a brandy syrup, perfectly grilled sardines, and the most tender, marinated octopus—

I forgot a girl singing as if Heaven was a mere breath away—

***

I forgot that, under his left eye, there lurked a scar people did not acknowledge but always culled from memory—

(I swiftly forgot "the 40 shades of grey" because before its utterance ended it was already a cliché.)

I forgot the dwarf Toulouse-Lautrec defining paradise as "a world of female odors and nerve endings"—

***

I forgot to freeze the spiral that is memory's perspective.

I forgot you losing all Alleluias.

I forgot Andalusia, where *duende* also insisted on "living life as if dreaming."

***

I forgot we accepted a colonizer's alphabet in exchange for electricity.

I forgot the classic contents of the Filipino Balikbayan Box:
Dove soap
L'Oreal shampoo
Colgate ("has to be Colgate, not Crest") toothpaste
SPAM corned beef

Set of *Encyclopedia Brittanica* from the 1970s
Nestle's Quick chocolate
Folger's (nowadays, Walmart house brand) coffee
Snickers
M&Ms
Irish Spring soap
Libby's corned beef
Costco Vitamin B-12
See's chocolates
Back issues of *Conde Nast Traveler, The New Yorker, Marie Claire,*
Entertainment Weekly, Newsweek, Glamour
Oil of Olay lotion Almay lotion Ziploc plastic bags Nutella
Reynolds aluminum foil and saran wrap
Campbell's soups
Nine West and Liz Claiborne purses ("from factory outlets") Parker
    pens with refills
Osh Kosh playsuit
Baby Gap, Old Navy and Fisher Price onesies
Bayer aspirin
Carnation instant creamer
Nail polish: "L'Oreal for family, Maybelline or Wet n Wild for the
    servants"
Shampoo: "Pantene for family, Suave for neighbors"

I forgot the incomplete narratives of remnants not yet borne away by
    birds, tiny animals, wind ...

***

I forgot wandering among the alleys of statistics for the *objectivity* lacking,
    claimed a dictator's daughter, in the criticism of her father.

I forgot ocean mirrors nothing but ocean.

I forgot the second-greatest among losses is disillusion.

***

I forgot the glint from the fang of a wild boar as he lurked behind even
    the most infinitesimal of shadows in a land where it only takes one
    domino to fall.

I forgot the elders, shoulders sagged to ruin, dropping gazes like debris instead of accommodating a world that drove them to treasure trees for providing shade that cost nothing.

I forgot mahogany dining tables whose royal lengths still failed to include me.

***

I forgot clutching the wet mane of a panicked horse.

Surely you walked through the spaces I hollowed from air and left behind in anticipation of you.

I forgot memory contains an underbrush.

***

I forgot black dimes interrupting the sun's glare, an experience familiar to travelers visiting "Namibia in search of pure light"—

I forgot you spilling vermouth on the sky.

I forgot ceasing our hurtle through the fragile chill of the Milky Way.

***

I forgot life defined through the credit card.

I forgot you reminding, "Honey, angels may fall but they never die."

I forgot lace.

***

I forgot that *piccola città* replete with hyphens.

I forgot the bare arms that defined "summer browned."

I forgot her red-rimmed eyes denoted the exhausted pace of a replicating light-year.

***

I forgot ink will flow to form a heart.

I forgot flamenco's First of Ten Commandments: *Dame la verdad,* Tell the Truth!

I forgot that when a stone hand cracks, its pieces will not be caught.

***

I forgot I wanted to make memories, not simply press petals between pages of expendable books.

I forgot the trip wire, leering as it hid in the shimmer of summer heat.

I forgot that "rehabilitation" meant he could accompany her smile that slid mirrors away from her eyes of blue sapphires.

***

I forgot a sea where I was immersed until, chin just topping salty water, my head became attached to the entire planet.

I forgot the color of your eyes which is grey.

I forgot Michelangelo possessed incomparable draftsmanship except as regards breasts, despite having been weaned by a daughter and wife of stone masons.

***

I forgot that meditation, if conducted deeply, must harvest pain.

All around the border of this place, the desert is a forever. I forgot how no mountains, no trees, no tomb markers—nor memories perfumed by jasmine—interrupted the horizon.

I forgot an archipelago where spaces between what are visible are as real as your body whose hands had raised my wedding veil.

***

I forgot prominent breasts sculpted on immobilized Virgin Marys. I forgot how one begins marking time from a lover's utterance of *Farewell*.

I forgot we once stood unknowingly in the same room of this city of numerous rooms—
did you frequent its space without knowing until now why you always looked intently at each face?

***

I forgot laughter is not comprised of stars.

I forgot the typhoon failing to decimate a landscape brimming with violet lilies, snapping turtles and fragile dandelions—

I forgot the neighbor hiding behind a curtain as he wrote a haiku about a thief tangoing with his shadow when the moon appeared.

From *Hiraeth: Tercets From
The Last Archipelago*, 2018

Flagging the Empty Flagpole

You were the altar that made me stay—Spine willingly
bent for a stranger's whip--Clutched the wet mane
of a panicked horse—The night was unanimous—

O erasure that captured the threshold of consciousness—
One begins marking time from a lover's utterance
of *Farewell*—A faux jasmine insists it *is* the scent of gold—

Even a boor pauses before a Rembrandt portrait—Mom
began to age when she began looking at the world through
heartbreaking resignation—Using color to prevent encounters

from degenerating into lies—Furious flamenco with vultures
under a menopausal sun—I was not an immigrant; I was
simply myself who lacked control at how the world formed

outside the "Other" of me—Rust taught me how bats operate
through radar—Plain bread can clear an oenophile's palate—
Her neck thinned until I could count the ropes stretched

along her throat—Admiring women who refuse to paint their lips—
Dust motes trapped in a tango after the sun lashed out a ray—
Bliss deep within an ascetic's eyes as he wandered with

a beggar's bowl—Your betrayal forever marks me like a heart
's tattoo blossoming painfully against an inner thigh—Limits
inevitable from mortality—Detachment can include; detachment

enabled a white rattlesnake to penetrate my dreams—The protect
-ion of his diamonds—Colors of a scream: the regret of crimson
the futility of pink, the astonishment of brown—To chafe at eating

food earned by someone else, each swallow bequeathing an
ineffable with the demeanor of ice—Your favorite color was water—
Picasso's Sleeping Nude, 1907: admirable for its lack

of sentimentality—Ache for fiction that does not chasten days—
A good day defined as eating a red apple while strolling
through white snow—New Mexico, where adobe walls were

soothed by brown paper bag lanterns glowing from lit candles—
~~Relief~~ Bliss defined as the liberating anonymity conferred
by travel: *Mindanao, Berlin, Melbourne, Amsterdam, Istanbul …*

become hours requiring no count—To become my own sculpture
when I crawled on a floor to see color from different angles—
Astonishment over a block of grey metal swallowing light—

The cocoon hung from a tree like a tender promise (I forgot
deferring judgment)—Obviating memory for a higher purpose—
Both perception and imperceptibility carry a price—

To be one of Michelangelo's slaves *surging* out of stone—History
defined as the World War II concentration camp where amnesiacs
tortured by tying together the legs of pregnant women—

Deflections enable a semblance of progress—Recognitions:
a white bird against a grey sky the same gesture I painted
for years as a single brushstroke of turquoise—Feeling you

in the air against my cheek—Your body against mine
introduced the limits of sunlight's expanse—Long for a sky
without horizon; instead, accede to the eye's clamor against

the opposite of claustrophobia—Jade's cousin: the green
of Antarctic berg ice a lost emerald rib broken and floating
away from a maternal continent—Addiction to *Duende* for

its intimacy with savagery—As an exposed nerve, you
greet mornings—Weariness defined as wishing to be pale—
Sky so lurid it was nonreverberative—To memorize

the marks of animals pawing as they hunt—Color has always
been a narrative—Preserving the capacity to feel you
in the breeze lifting my hair from their shyness—

English's Wandering Authenticity

I.
The world saw me as a humpback—Your hands paused
before my black brassiere—"Honey, angels fall but
they never die"—To be an angel is to be alone in a smudged

gown, fingers poking through holes burnt by epistemology—
Drinking from ancient goblets whose cracked rims snagged
lips into a bleeding burning, I forgot my flesh was ruin—

II.
A baby rattlesnake stained the asphalt green, smashed
by a neighbor who, it was rumored, adored massive mahogany
libraries jam-packed with cracked leather covers, yellowing

pages, and wisdom best left forgotten—A big-bellied man
whispered *Murder can remain mere story* over a cigar
smoked down to the length of my then-enchanting thumb—

III.
Birds formed a toupee for trees—Violet bruises from a rifle's
intimacy—Trauma defined as the hollows formed when
knees bent, then kneeled—A girl shrieked as her swing

soared towards a boiling sky—Feet mischievously walking
two inches above ground—Belting my jeans with a used halo—
A pedestal bloodied by ~~what~~ who leapt from it—Envying

IV.
thorns—Beauty can be reasonable if one tolerates boredom—
Fear is a loss—Vivid is subjective—A poet insisted, "abashed
aubergine"—A Bengal Tiger mimicking a helicopter's dance—

Lineage seduces—Manolo Blahnik's faux elegy for crocodiles—
The momentary immortality of a new car—Oxymoron defined
as "Mutual Funds"—Cheer dispersed through fishnet stockings—

V.
Dusk enhancing conversations—Plankton beneath the wave
radiating from green to gold with the onset of wet sunlight—
Desire ascending when it rains—A white azalea quieted shade

into a girl—A girl loved marble enough to freeze into a swoon—
Skin of jasmine mirroring sky—Preening over a labyrinth—
You there with blue veins cracking transparent membrane—

VI.
The weaver elongating holes into tears—The empress hum
-ing calculus—Symmetries shaped by memory lapses—
He learned her body as a white finger holding back starlight—

Accepting a colonizer's alphabet for electricity—Defining
ambition as helpless, like a compulsion to write songs for
women who will never wear headscarves—That wandering

VII.
authenticity—The air of a country where the love for a woman
is the love for a man is the love for Allah! Mohammed welcoming
Jews and Christians for they, too, are "People of the Book"—

Where the Pages End

For someone sighted in a dream, she released milk
for orphaned baby birds—It was not a blood teardrop
but the last red pepper hanging from a string

in front of a white wall—Water became like love:
miserable and lovely—Memory contains an under
-brush—The inevitability of ashes—Revelation as

a water lily forming instantaneously—Laughter
comprised of stars—It seemed the sun hummed
along—That plasticity of recognition: silk, moonlight,

velvet, crème brulee, honey on fingertip, awkward
blood—Pride more adept than eye in discerning
the invisible—The religions of flocks with tin feathers—

Audacity, at times, must be a private affair—Birthland
defined as an island replete with chastened alleyways—
Sentences like veins—The Introduction as a permanent

state—Romance emanating from someone else's summer
-dusted landscape—The relish of pronunciation:
"Burkina Faso"—You were drowning in the Seychelles

relishing the uncomprehended word: "Seychelles"—
Gardenias crushed for perfume entrusted with
cancelling midnights—Tentative acacia trees waiting

behind sand dunes—You defined as *that* sense of
approaching a labyrinth—Fate defined as your mouth
become a cave stuffed with another woman's hair—

Kapwa's Song

—for Leny M. Strobel

I.
Evening musk quivering into post-elegance—Blossoming
of desk lamps—I wanted to make memories, not press
petals between pages of ancient books—Someone pleaded

to be buried under a canopy of red roses—No need to
apologize for dancing from one's hips *roundly*, eyes closed
taking up as much space as one wants on the dance floor

of someone else's wedding—When Pygmalion sculpted
himself into an embrace he used stone in hopes the hold
would never break—Sand shimmering with black diamonds

the world pausing to form a black diamond, fear becoming
as real as a black diamond—Ancient warriors captured
the brutality of cracked skies through "lightning marks"

as long grooves along the wooden shafts of their arrows—
Feel votive candle flickering within navel—Montana, where
you breathed *deeply* the scent of black earth, *dampening…*

and becoming a forever metaphor—O practicality of water—
Wasp nesting behind screen door—Whispering to a daughter
borne from rape, "Regret is not your legacy"—Violets vomiting

rue—O storm shaming me for watering the nasturtiums all
summer with dishwater—Agony of knowing no aftermath
after recognizing what made you rear up on your death bed—

Mental snapshot of three coyotes goldened by sunlight
as they peed upon the buttercups—Wrestling a long poem until
all thorns have been gathered into cupped palms for birthing

psalms (O smile at a stranger's blood mixed with rose petals
for generous perfume)—Turquoise on the Kachina doll hanging
on your wall, color of sunlit ocean embracing Greece while you

explored Mexico: I remember Philip Lamantia—Puzzle of
agriculture: Philip Lamantia entering the blue frame of glass
bordering the blue wooden door into *Maykadeh* where we met

for "they do wonders with tongue." Sprezzatura woke my veins—
How, sweetly, you offered eggplant, its skin made palatable
through much prior bruising: I remember you, Philip Lamantia—

II.
I forgot my birth language Ilokano: *maysa, duwa, tallo, upat,*
lima, inem, pito, walo, siam, sangapulo… Allow diamonds
to fray—Maturity defined as recognizing the second-greatest

loss is disillusion—Look at the decaying world through slitted
eyes—When the hunched sommelier corrected, "You mean
'saddle leather'," I learned one can forget what one never knew—

Define the figure eight as an hourglass frittering time away—
Icarus actually lived and the sky went livid—Red pistils rising
from waxy white petals always look profane and magnificent

-ly divine—Blades tangoed on my palms to carve life-lines—
Wings curled beneath black leather—A "someday" as
elusive as a cab at 4 a.m., and the musky scent of fortitude—

O crushing tune that worked Baudelaire to the bone—Waiting
by grimy hotel glass, peeking through hair, fingering lace
sleeves, envying the lobby's silk flowers for their inability to feel—

White birch flashing through forest greenery evoked your eyes—
Duende that overcomes without satiating the longing for more—
Derrida hunched as I was over an antique desk scribbling past

egregious back pain, "There is speech. / There is phenomena."
—Athena also rises from the gape of wounds—

III.

Charisma defined

as a wall at dusk with shelves of books whose spines stared
at you as a neighbor's saxophone elongated a note from low to
high to low—Your finger tracing the cheek I offered as proxy—

How the ellipsis hides, elides, gives up … Forgotten orphan, skinny
as he offered his toys: twigs, cracked stone, two matchboxes
cradling spiders, earthworm in tin can—Pounding through fields

of tall grass to release the beauty of white butterflies rising in a panic—
Abu Ghraib—Tondo, a shanty town created by a massive garbage
dump called "Smokey Mountain"—Mountains losing trees for books

about mountains losing trees—Kali warriors memorizing *halad*
to quicken the surfacing of deadly positions during hours of battle—
A yellowed photograph slipping from brittle pages—Milk leaking

from the corner of the sleeping child's mouth—Believing the world
was overpopulated by mothers who would always welcome back
prodigal sons and daughters with warm rice and cool slices of

pineapple—Sarong undoing itself to the trill of birdsong—Sarong's
fall bringing down the eagle with curious eyes—Sarong caressed
breasts and thighs before it was borne away by a river's current—

Sarong fell and a river blushed—*Ikaw, aking pag-ibig, ay naruon…*
"You, my Love, were there…"

IV.

O stone garden in Kyoto where the 15th
stone is invisible from all angles—That the sun practices justice by

privileging vines which work harder on steep terrain amid gravel
than on level land fertile with natural nutrients and easily accessed
by water—Kathmandu where I recognized you in me and I in you

upon turning a street corner onto a plaza where every inch was
topped by mud pots, their inky glazes like benefactions from goats
peering through second- and third-story windows—Coltrane in Napa

Valley, his "Pursuance" the rhythm of your heartbeat against my
roaming palm, and the sound of grapevines growing—A flock of
starlings shattering the sky's clean plate like grains of black pepper—

A calf affixed to an iron rotisserie: the animal cooked slowly for hours.
and hours until its meat was a page-turn away from falling from the
bone—A valley witnessing my return to you with a primitive ardor

shared by hunting hawks, crack of cartilage audible as they
obviated distance, as they swooped, wings flared as if posing
for Rembrandt—O those paintings that evoke what lives outside

the frame, like a woman who so loved a man she ate his testicles
between quaffs of sweet jerez, chewing and chewing meat before
swallowing—

V.

A tremor ripples a vein in anticipation of a possibility.

Another possibility: a tremor ripples a vein in anticipation—We
never knew the opposite of *Easy Beauty*—Darkness was the key
not the lock—A wooden door in Ulan Ude, cracked in places

a wash of faded blue paint tattooed by pale green diamonds
evoking island in the Sulu Sea, an emerald floating on lapis lazuli
staining, too, the sky—A night train lumbering across Siberia in

whose hold Ivan, a Russian geologist, apologized for his poor
English by reciting Pushkin in his native tongue. Ezra Pound was
correct: inarticulate sounds transport as music—A room where

the only sign of contentment was a gown framed on one wall
its dance present but not visible—Ignoring Paris waiting on
the other side of a shuttered window—Passion always exacts

a price, and Love is always eager to pay—A beach where
sand constantly shifted its hollows—The debris from attempting to
unify "the convex with the concave"—Writing a poem, then turning

it physical (I forgot its opposite is equally arduous…and lyrical)—
A girl singing as if Heaven was mere breath away—A girl singing
to repel a black bear—A girl singing along with Dave Brubeck

after he regaled with a tale: he turned to music only after studying
how to heal cattle as a vet. I forgot Dave Brubeck on the piano,
Randy Jones on drums, Jack Six on string bass, Bobby Militello on

sax—all conspiring for "The Time of Our Madness"—

VI.
                                                              A girl singing
to mountains in Nepal quivering like 500-pound Sumo wrestlers—
A girl singing to *la luna naranja*—A girl singing as she spun a globe,

its whirl evoking the guarantee of returns with all departures—A girl
singing *I will become Babaylan!* with notes only virgin boys can
muster, only dogs can hear—A girl singing to unfurl wings that have

never betrayed her—A girl singing as she smooched the sun… A girl
singing forth her benedictions: May you never grow intimate with cold
ashes and burlap. May you never feel tar and black feathers. May

you know what I saw through *flames*… A girl singing in Porto Vecchio:
lobster at noon, a tiny tortoise tip-toeing across the bedspread, a bus
endearingly halted by determined partridges marching across the road

as Simone De Beauvoir and Nelson Algren watched—Heaven could
be … a breath away—I am trying to remember how a girl clung to
herself, how she persevered to remain in constant song—

IV. DEATH POEMS

> *... the story can be revealed only if the participant-turned-documenter is willing to undergo the suffering that truth-telling requires. Once, a poet observed, "The deepest meditation must require the self-infliction of unrelenting anguish."*
> —*from* DoveLion, *a novel by Eileen R. Tabios*

Dear A, This Poem Is Not For You

I caress you knowing you soon will be dead.
I will have emptied the syringe.
I defined kindness by ordering you sedated before I injected the poison.

I wanted to kill you quickly and my husband disagreed.
Just two more days, he insisted.
Give me more time to say goodbye … as if there is ever enough time to say
    goodbye.

I disagreed, but couplehood is a dance requiring a *willingness* by both
    participants.
I wanted to kill you quickly.
For my husband, I let you live two more days.

My husband had a plan.
He wanted to feed you something you've never been allowed to eat—he
    wanted you to experience one more new treat.
His plan called for rare roast beef.

I bought four pounds as, for you, I could be generous.
Though I wanted you dead, I was the one who brought you this delicacy.
In the category of "gods are cruel" or "gods have a sense of humor,"
    you turned away from the meat whose unfamiliarity, you assumed,
    masked more drugs.

You were tired of your drugs.
I was tired of your drugs.
My husband was tired of your drugs: Tramadol, Terbinafine, Carprofen,
    Tylosin, Noxafil, Pepcid, Vitamin B12, and all the others which
    were not effective (Mycafungin, Posaconazole, Diphenhydramine,
    Cyproheptadine, Phellostatin, Back Support Herbal Supplement …)

Fortunately, the cats like roast beef so your treat will not go to waste.
I could feed it to the other dogs but they also eat single-protein diets to
    maximize health and their protein is currently turkey.

But let it be said, even if the meat had been tossed into the forest, I would not have begrudged its expense.

Then night approached.
I put you to bed.
You liked to sleep on the rug by my computer in the kitchen where I write poems—where I am writing this poem, not for you (though you soon will be dead) but for my husband.

I woke up the next morning to the thought that, soon, you will be dead.
I rushed to the kitchen to maximize my time with you but you were not there.
I looked around, starting to panic, as you were not where you should have been as you have been for years.

I walked swiftly through the house and found you waiting for me at the foot of the staircase.
Sometime during the night, you had fallen down its steps.
With your deteriorated spine it's a miracle your back did not break multiple times.

You had peed, copiously, on the rug.
But never mind that—
You soon will be dead.

I grieved as I knew that, sometime during the dark—and there is no black like starless rural darkness—you must have woken and became confused.
You must have struggled upright though your two back legs no longer supported your otherwise magnificent body.
Confused, you must have wandered through the black before falling into an abyss you could not see.

Confused, you could not leave where your bladder emptied itself out in a wave that, later, will cause me to destroy a rug that's warmed our home for three decades.
Confused, you kept company with your urine until morning brought me to you.
Confused, you must have been ashamed as the latest scientific studies contradict long-held beliefs that dogs are not self-aware.

Losing dignity is painful.
Watching someone lose dignity is painful.
Neither is as painful as when you soon will die, cradled in my weary arms.

My husband had a plan.
Forced out of town for a day, he asked me to implement his plan.
His plan caused you to wake up to darkness, fall down a staircase in
    confusion, and stay mired in pee until dawn brought me to find you.

Should I tell my husband the cost of his plan to give you one last treat?
Should I leave the information in this poem knowing he does not read all
    of the poems written by prolific me?
This poem is for him, not you who soon will be dead and deserves a
    different type of poem—a poem that involves zero guilt and a basket
    of beloved kittens.

Yes, I shall bury the information in this poem.
My husband had a plan birthed from kindness as he is a kind man.
Kindness cannot protect everyone from everything all of the time.

Kindness may not protect against the costs of hope.
Kindness cannot protect against all of grief's manifestations.
Such, is the insult to the injury of your brief life span: there are limits to
    kindness.

Hay(na)ku Death Poems (2018-2019)

—written in the "reverse hay(na)ku" form to visually manifest disappearance

#1
Onions are burning—
smoke becomes
sweet

#2
Familiar, joyous barking—
we'll meet
again

#3
My ears ring
singing no
song

#4
Veins rippling protests—
rivers into
Hades

#5
Veins carving rivers
traversing blue
sky

where
no angel
spreads its wings

#6
Veins etching body—
landscape of
regret

#7
As studies show
grief overcomes
joy

on one's deathbed

#8
To be human
is to
sin.

But knowledge is
no palliative
upon

reaching one's deathbed

#9
I wrote poems
as babies
suffered.

Babies suffered as
I wrote
poems

#10
Babies suffered as
I wrote
poems

on writing poems
as babies
suffered

#11
Making poems out
of failures
does

not redeem anything.
For that?
Forgiveness

#12

—*after "Tahlequah is still carrying her dead calf, for a 16th straight day, and researchers fear she could be in danger" by Lynda V. Mapes, Seattle Times, Aug. 8-9, 2018*

Did I live
a life
worth

the weight of
my corpse
upon

a mother weakening
but still
carrying

carrying carrying carrying
carrying carrying
caring

#13

—*for Aretha Franklin, Aug. 16, 2018*

Through the bad
rhymes we
reached

a place where
there's no
space

or time and
now I
sing

this song for
you, replete
with

love no longer
hiding. I'm
singing

this song for
you. I'm
singing

#14
Against silence, even
haiku are
maximalists

#15
From your vantage
point, windows
bring

in the outside
for your
enjoyment

until the bird
crashes against
such

a clear pane
windexed for
clarity—

You are reminded
of your
cruel

hypocrisy in creating
this bloody
Anthropocene

#16

*Written during the 2018 U.S. Senate hearings regarding the nomination of Judge
James Kavanaugh to the Supreme Court.*

"Himpathy"—an awful
word, yet
accurate

note from violins
playing while
burning

#17

Nightingale floors

I've always felt
Beauty can
deter

death, even before
I discovered
nightingale

floors at Nijo-jo
Castle chirping
alarms

against Ninja assassins
solidifying the
shadows.

The nightingale does
not always
sing

as if perched
on branches
dripping

pink blossoms on
wet gray
gravel.

"For prosperity, let
all senses
see,"

this old woman
cackles with
glee

#18
You never wanted
to live
long

enough to be
surprised by
Faith

#19

How I Learned to Draw A Circle

1.
He fed me
olives and
Portuguese

wine. What else
might you
desire

from life when
you've received
this

moment good enough
to serve
as

epitaph: "Philip Lamantia
served her
olives

and Portuguese wine"—
a great
moment

and only one
of many.
Thus,

why still be
consumed by
Desire?

2.
Philip never stopped
writing poems,
unlike

other poets who
aged into
prose.

And when you
complained over
your

inability to draw
a straight
line

he insisted, "Then
draw a
curve!"

NOTES

147 Million Orphans
A haybun is one of hay(na)ku's variations: a combination of tercet and prose. *147 Million Orphans* is the first book publication of haybuns.

Dredging For Atlantis
"The Bread of Florence"
The poem was inspired by Kinta Beevor's memoir, *A Tuscan Childhood* (Pantheon Books, New York, 1993).

Footnotes to Algebra: Uncollected Poems 1995-2009
"Montana: A Novel" and "Ellen: Chapter 2" utilizes texts partly annotated from *Winter Wheat*, a resonant novel by Mildred Walker (University of Nebraska Press, Lincoln and London, 1992).

The series, "Girl Singing," was inspired by Jose Garcia Villa's poem "Girl Singing. Day". The series was written during an artist residency at Villa Montalvo, California. Also, the series' "The Secret Life of An Angel" became the root-source for 151 multi-genre translations and responses from 47 poets worldwide collected in *1000 Views of "Girl Singing"*, Editor John Bloomberg-Rissman (Leafe Press, U.K., 2009).

Hay(na)ku Death Poems
The series was written after "Retirement Poem," a journal entry-as-poem written out of weariness with the poetry world:

Retirement Poem

"I used to think a poem should sing; now I think a poem should think"
—*Jose Garcia Villa*

So you hit that age / when you can look back / and reconsider / a life—your life

Making money to make / rent food clothes utilities / etcetera etcetera happen / can allow one to believe / one did something worthwhile

The problem with doing / something that does not / make money is that the act / highlights the act itself

—in this case writing poems—

for the inevitable question: / *Are the poems any good?*

which is to say, *Was this life / of making poems ... any good?*

Perhaps a poet anticipates this / almost clichetic (re-)consideration

But to embark on a path of questions / means there always will be / at least one unexpected question:

> *Even if the poems are good / was the life of making them … / good enough? / Today a President / forced a baby to go to court / to answer a different question: / Why are you here, uninvited?*

The baby reached out tiny hands / No one moved to hug him / Of such moments are cruel / Presidents made—a poet / might call this "another cliché"

An ending like this is how poets / earn their value: a reader may / leave for the courthouse to protest / by offering the baby a hug before / answering on behalf of the baby

Children are always invited / A nation does not become strong / pretending to be a cocktail party / with a four-figure admission fee

Later, the President would be kicked / out of the house he had darkened / a house created from the hopes / of many babies, a white house / because babies only know light— / the first thing they see when / they enter a world that will / introduce them to cruelty, but

also contain a poet who wrote / "Poetry is not words" / and readers who read such words / to shut the book, turn off computers / and leave their homes to make / a more hospitable, inviting world

"Hay(na)ku Death Poem #18"

Written Nov. 13, 2018 during the author's Jury Duty experience in Napa, California which opened with one of the local judges greeting the summoned jurors. The judge (whose name I can't recall) said that a judge usually welcomed potential jurors during the first day of their summoned duty. During such welcome speeches, jurors often shared some little-known facts about the courts, the legal system, jury duty, etc. But this day, this judge—who also said "I'm usually funnier"—said he didn't feel like making light talk given the times: the recent mass shootings as well as the wildfires now burning at both ends of California. But he also said that it was specifically during these rough times that he came to appreciate more our legal system—that it is a way, during tough times, of trying to work things out and hopefully work things out fairly. I was surprised to be moved by his faith … and, more specifically and significantly, saddened that I was surprised to be moved by anyone nowadays expressing faith. For the poem's purpose, *"Compassion"* was the trait raised in the first draft, before realizing that *"Faith"* is more true to its underlying inspiration.

Hiraeth: Tercets From the Last Archipelago
"Kapwa's Song"

Kapwa is a Filipino cultural concept of interconnectedness whereby other people are not "others" but part of what one is. What others say:

> … the tendency to see the world with all its beings as a holistic system

where things operate interdependently. Harmony with other people and the environment is a much-needed trait today in our shrinking global village. This orientation is called "kapwa"—the shared self — in the Filipino traditional value system
—Leny M. Strobel

Being Filipina isn't defined only by what I do as an individual, but by the living, breathingness of Kapwa that takes into account my environment, my choices, the choices of others, my fears and triumphs, all at the same time, all in constant motion.
—Rebecca Mabanglo-Mayor

The phrase "O practicality of water" is written appreciatively after Brenda Hillman's *Practical Water* (Wesleyan Poetry Series, 2009).

Menopausal Hay(na)ku for P-Grubbers
"Hay Naku! That Menopause!"
This chained hay(na)ku sequence was inspired by the article "The Truth is Out There (About Menopause)" by Gillian Anderson and Jennifer Nadel, *LENNY*, March 7, 2017. Some lines quote or paraphrase from the article.

Nota Bene Eiswein
The poems were each written after each of the poems in Christian Hawkey's poetry collection, *The Book of Funnels* (Wave Books, Seattle, WA, 2007). Each poem began as a riff from the ending of a Hawkey poem … and went on from there.

The Light Sang As It Left Your Eyes: Our Autobiography
"Ifugao Red"
"Ifugao" refers to a native tribe in the Luzon mountain region and Pampanga province in the Philippines. The poem was first published in the anthology *SAINTS OF HYSTERIA: A Half-Century of Collaborative American Poetry*, Editors Denise Duhamel, Maureen Seaton, and David Trinidad (Brooklyn, Soft Skull Press, 2006). The poem appeared in the anthology with this "process note":

> Filipino and Filipino-American poets have been the bastard children of American poetry for more than a hundred years, spawned by the U.S. invasion of the Philippines in 1898. Although often overlooked, marginalized, disinherited, alienated, or forgotten, this rich tradition of poetry is worthy of inclusion in the main fabric of American and English literature.

> Thus, Nick Carbo and Eileen Tabios collaborate on poems which include references to Filipino culture. It is their hope that non-Filipino readers read the poems and be moved to research the Filipino references (in the same way that readers are asked to research Greek, French and other Eurocentric or Western references frequently inserted in poems that make up the literary canon), thereby learning about Filipino culture.

> The collaborative nature of authorship also relates to their

consciousness that English was a colonizing tool in the Philippines. Following the U.S. military invasion in 1898, English spread across the archipelago to solidify their imperialist rule to become the preferred language for commerce, education and politics. When Carbo and Tabios collaborate together to write poems, they do so partly to shield their autobiographical "I"s as forming the authors of these poems. For these poems are written in English.

On "Ifugao Red," the poets collaborated through email. Carbo recollects: "One line you. One line me. One comma here. One ellipsis there. Is that my vergule dangling from your page? Ah, the ampersand has spoken and! You spun your tilde on the table."

"Maganda Begins"
The poem was inspired by John Banville's novel, *Athena* (Vintage Books, New York, 1995).

The Singer and Others: Flamenco Hay(na)ku
The poems reflect my imagined application of two techniques upon Sarah Bird's inspiring novel, *The Flamenco Academy* (Knopf, New York, 2006): the painterly technique of scumbling and the "fish-ing" process of Filipinos picking words from the language of Spanish colonizers and using them differently (e.g. as puns) from the words' original definitions, as described in Vicente L. Rafael's *Contracting Colonialism: Translation and Christian Conversion in Tagalog Society Under Early Spanish Rule* (Duke University Press, 1993).

"La Loca"
The epigraph is a hay(na)ku translation of the first two stanzas of Federico Garcia Lorca's poem "Ditty of First Desire."

On Green Lawn, The Scent of White
The mini-book-length poem was written while reading *Commander In Chief* (A Jack Ryan Novel) by Tom Clancy and Mark Greaney (G.P. Putnam's Sons, 2015)

To Be An Empire Is to Burn
"Ferdinand Edralin Marcos"
The poem is written in the "Rippled Mirror Hay(na)ku" form: two stanzas where the basic hay(na)ku tercet is followed by a reverse hay(na)ku tercet and where the second tercet's narrative almost mirrors the first tercet's.

Your Father Is Bald: Selected Hay(na)ku Poems
"The Ineffability of Mushrooms (A Novella-in-Verse)"
The poem was inspired by Kinta Beevor's memoir, *A Tuscan Childhood* (Pantheon Books, New York, 1993).

ABOUT THE POET

Eileen R. Tabios has released over 50 collections of poetry, fiction, essays, and experimental biographies from publishers in nine countries and cyberspace. Her books include a form-based "Selected Poems" series, *The In(ter)vention of the Hay(na)ku: Selected Tercets 1996-2019*, *THE GREAT AMERICAN NOVEL: Selected Visual Poetry (2001-2019)*, *INVENT(ST)ORY: Selected Catalog Poems & New 1996-2015*, and *THE THORN ROSARY: Selected Prose Poems & New 1998-2010*. She's also released the first book-length haybun collection, *147 MILLION ORPHANS (MMXI-MML)*; a collected novels, *SILK EGG*; an experimental autobiography *AGAINST MISANTHROPY*; as well as two bilingual and one trilingual editions involving English, Spanish and Romanian. Her award-winning body of work includes invention of the hay(na)ku poetic form (whose 15-year anniversary in 2018 was celebrated in the U.S. with exhibitions, a new anthology, and readings at the San Francisco \ and St. Helena Public Libraries as well as a first poetry book, *BEYOND LIFE SENTENCES* (1998), which received the Philippines' National Book Award for Poetry. Translated into ten languages, she also has edited, co-edited or conceptualized 15 anthologies of poetry, fiction and essays, as well as exhibited visual art in the United States, Philippines, Malaysia, and Serbia. Her writing and editing works have received recognition through awards, grants and residencies. More information is available at http://eileenrtabios.com

Titles from Marsh Hawk Press

Jane Augustine *Arbor Vitae; Krazy: Visual Poems and Performance Scripts; Night Lights; A Woman's Guide to Mountain Climbing*
Tom Beckett *Dipstick (Diptych)*
Sigman Byrd *Under the Wanderer's Star*
Patricia Carlin *Original Green; Quantum Jitters; Second Nature*
Claudia Carlson *The Elephant House; My Chocolate Sarcophagus; Pocket Park*
Meredith Cole *Miniatures*
Jon Curley *Hybrid Moments; Scorch Marks*
Neil de la Flor *Almost Dorothy; An Elephant's Memory of Blizzards*
Chard deNiord *Sharp Golden Thorn*
Sharon Dolin *Serious Pink*
Steve Fellner *Blind Date with Cavafy; The Weary World Rejoices*
Thomas Fink *Selected Poems & Poetic Series; Joyride; Peace Conference; Clarity and Other Poems; After Taxes; Gossip*
Norman Finkelstein *Inside the Ghost Factory; Passing Over*
Edward Foster *The Beginning of Sorrows; Dire Straits; Mahrem: Things Men Should Do for Men; Sewing the Wind; What He Ought to Know*
Paolo Javier *The Feeling is Actual*
Burt Kimmelman *Abandoned Angel; Somehow*

Burt Kimmelman and Fred Caruso *The Pond at Cape May Point*
Basil King *The Spoken Word / The Painted Hand from Learning to Draw / A History; 77 Beasts: Basil King's Beastiary; Mirage*
Martha King *Imperfect Fit*
Phillip Lopate *At the End of the Day: Selected Poems and An Introductory Essay*
Mary Mackey *Breaking the Fever; The Jaguars That Prowl Our Dreams; Sugar Zone; Travelers With No Ticket Home*
Jason McCall *Dear Hero,*
Sandy McIntosh *The After-Death History of My Mother; Between Earth and Sky; Cemetery Chess; Ernesta, in the Style of the Flamenco; Forty-Nine Guaranteed Ways to Escape Death; A Hole In the Ocean: A Hamptons' Apprenticeship; Lesser Lights: More Tales from a Hamptons' Apprenticeship; Obsessional*
Stephen Paul Miller *Any Lie You Tell Will Be the Truth; The Bee Flies in May; Fort Dad; Skinny Eighth Avenue; There's Only One God and You're Not It*
Daniel Morris *Bryce Passage; Hit Play; If Not for the Courage*
Geoffrey O'Brien *The Blue Hill*
Sharon Olinka *The Good City*
Christina Olivares *No Map of the Earth Includes Stars*
Justin Petropoulos *Eminent Domain*

Paul Pines *Charlotte Songs; Divine Madness; Gathering Sparks; Last Call at the Tin Palace*
Jacquelyn Pope *Watermark*
George Quasha *Things Done for Themselves*
Karin Randolph *Either She Was*
Rochelle Ratner *Balancing Acts; Ben Casey Days; House and Home*
Michael Rerick *In Ways Impossible to Fold*
Corrine Robins *Facing It; One Thousand Years; Today's Menu*
Eileen R. Tabios *The Connoisseur of Alleys; I Take Thee, English, for My Beloved; The In(ter)vention of the Hay(na)ku: Selected Tercets (1996-2019); The Light Sang as It Left Your Eyes: Our Autobiography; Reproductions of the Empty Flagpole; Sun Stigmata; The Thorn Rosary*
Eileen R. Tabios and j/j hastain *The Relational Elations of Orphaned Algebra*
Susan Terris *Familiar Tense; Ghost of Yesterday; Natural Defenses*
Lynne Thompson *Fretwork*
Madeline Tiger *Birds of Sorrow and Joy*
Tana Jean Welch *Latest Volcano*
Harriet Zinnes *Drawing on the Wall; Light Light or the Curvature of the Earth; New and Selected Poems; Weather is Whether; Whither Nonstopping*

YEAR	AUTHOR	MHP POETRY PRIZE TITLE	JUDGE
2004	Jacquelyn Pope	*Watermark*	Marie Ponsot
2005	Sigman Byrd	*Under the Wanderer's Star*	Gerald Stern
2006	Steve Fellner	*Blind Date with Cavafy*	Denise Duhamel
2007	Karin Randolph	*Either She Was*	David Shapiro
2008	Michael Rerick	*In Ways Impossible to Fold*	Thylias Moss
2009	Neil de la Flor	*Almost Dorothy*	Forrest Gander
2010	Justin Petropoulos	*Eminent Domain*	Anne Waldman
2011	Meredith Cole	*Miniatures*	Alicia Ostriker
2012	Jason McCall	*Dear Hero,*	Cornelius Eady
2013	Tom Beckett	*Dipstick (Diptych)*	Charles Bernstein
2014	Christina Olivares	*No Map of the Earth Includes Stars*	Brenda Hillman
2015	Tana Jean Welch	*Latest Volcano*	Stephanie Strickland
2016	Robert Gibb	*After*	Mark Doty
2017	Geoffrey O'Brien	*The Blue Hill*	Meena Alexander
2018	Lynne Thompson	*Fretwork*	Jane Hirshfield

Artistic Advisory Board
Toi Derricotte, Denise Duhamel, Marilyn Hacker, Allan Kornblum (in memorium), Maria Mazzioti Gillan, Alicia Ostriker, Marie Ponsot, David Shapiro, Nathaniel Tarn, Anne Waldman, and John Yau.

For more information, please go to: **www.marshhawkpress.org**